EXPERIENCES IN BUILDING AND LEADING A PMO

EXPERIENCES IN BUILDING AND LEADING A PMO

Best Practices in a Centralized Program Management Office

Karen M. Marks

ISBN: 0692939075
ISBN 13: 9780692939079
Library of Congress Control Number: 2017912941
Peak Method Consulting, Las Vegas, NV

DEDICATION

For Jim – none of this was possible without you

ACKNOWLEDGEMENTS

I would like to thank a few individuals who helped to make this book a reality, and while many of these people are no longer with us, their impact on me has shaped the career that I had and the person I am today.

My husband Jim, to whom this book is dedicated, is the most supportive and loving partner any woman could ask for. He has let me soar, and yet has always been there to catch me when I fall.

My mother Evelyn, so far ahead of her time, a controller for a gas company back in the 1960's, working full time and knowingly working for less money than her male counterparts, she was my role model, taught me what work ethic means, and made me believe that I could be anything I wanted to be, and I know she watches over me today.

My father Billy, his own story of early baseball and WWII would fill a book too. You were a wonderful and fun dad who gave me my love of sports.

My sister Kathy, I miss you so much, and I am forever grateful that we were so close. The second mother to my children, the voice of reason and calm, you did so much for me all my life. You are always with me.

My children Jessica and Matthew and my granddaughters Amarah and Revennah – still my pride and inspiration – and motivation!!

My mentors, the late Mrs. Elizabeth Marsh, Paul Feldman, the late Kathy Staffaroni, thank you for your wisdom, guidance and your friendship.

PMO Champion and friend, Dr. Marcus Schabacker – thank you for your vision, support and ongoing encouragement.

PREFACE

Like most readers, when I choose a "how to" book, I have always preferred a book that gets quickly to the heart of what I'm looking for, right to the "how" part, rather than a major dissertation of the author's experiences and anecdotes. This book is written for individuals familiar with Project Management and having a solid understanding of many of the hurdles that project managers face on a regular basis.

This book is also a culmination of over 35 years of business experience in multiple companies and from working in and ultimately leading various shapes and sizes of Program Management Offices (PMO's) along the way, in both a centralized and decentralized model. While I am sure to include some of my experiences and anecdotes, my intention is to give you a roadmap of best practices and a balance of ideas that will work for any size or type PMO, in any company, regardless of industry. That said, I should note that in the Pharmaceutical or Medical Device industry, there are many regulations that Project Managers need to understand, navigate and comply with, that Project Managers in the telecommunications, IT or other industries do not. Each industry brings its own special requirements.

Surprisingly, you will find that I am not a purist when it comes to Project Management. There is a guidance that needs to be followed, a common-sense outline that allows flexibility, because as we all know, all projects are not created equal. In Project Management, one size (or one style) does not fit all.

Nothing happens overnight, and while there are a lot of ideas, tools and processes included in this book, choose wisely as to which options are best for you to implement first based on the needs and the culture of the company you work for. You can't implement all of these items at the same time. It's overwhelming to you, your team and the rest of the organization. Look for the quick wins, recognize that change happens slowly in some companies, and take the time to plan and pilot all implementation activities and measure the outcomes of the early initiatives that you select. You will have better success in the long run if you first build your relationships, gain agreement for your plan, and then pilot the implementation of the selected items that will work best for your organization.

Those who know me well will tell you that I am straightforward, blunt and do not speak for the sake of hearing my own voice. I'm finding my writing style to be much the same. While I do go into depth on each of the topics, it may not be deep enough for some of you. At the end of the book, I provide my contact information if you would like further detail, yet I am also hoping that many of you will find your own ideas in these pages, using this book as a guide and assessing what your specific company needs and what your company's culture will tolerate, and then crafting and building upon these ideas and tools to fit those needs within the company and industry where you work today......or tomorrow!

TABLE OF CONTENTS -- CHAPTERS

CHAPTER 1

VARIABLES

There are a few variables that ultimately define the success or failure of a Project Management Office. First and foremost, is support from the highest levels in the organization. Without this level of support and commitment behind a PMO, whether in the form of a well-placed individual champion, or multiple Executive Committee members who are willing to take a chance on forming a true, centralized PMO, the effort will be ultimately wasted.

In most companies today, project managers exist in multiple functions and not in a cohesive or managed group. In this common scenario, project managers work primarily towards the objectives of the functions they support, and clearly have a stake (their ongoing employment) in that specific function. The danger in that is that all outcomes are skewed to the benefit of the function that they reside in. There is little to no objectivity in discussing or addressing the problems that may be living in the project due to that function's lack of capabilities, or lack of willingness to address their own shortcomings.

In a centralized PMO, all problems and issues are on the table, with full objectivity from the PMO since by virtue of the stand-alone nature of the PMO, that becomes the job – to be the source of truth in the project and to hold all functions, including the PMO, accountable for the results of the project.

Not all C-suite level executives know or have seen the value of a PMO. In fact, in many cases, most only see Project Managers in a "clerical" role, someone who takes notes or pulls together timelines and project plans, rather than well-trained leaders who know how to motivate a team, plan a project, identify critical risks and ultimately execute and deliver a successful project launch.

Progressive and informed executives, within the right corporate culture, will not see a centralized PMO as a power wielding entity that ties up money and resources, but in its true capacity of an objective organization whose entire purpose is to develop and execute the product pipeline for the company into vital and revenue producing products.

The second variable to the success of a PMO lies within the culture of the company. Try to define where the focus lies within the company – is it an R&D (Research and Development) driven company or a commercially (Marketing) driven company? Are there good relationships between Manufacturing, R&D and Marketing? Who is holding the purse strings? How much competition is there between the functions? How large are the existing project teams? How well do the senior leaders get along? Each one of the above questions will provide you with important clues as to whether or not a centralized PMO can or cannot be successful within the company.

A company that has good internal cross-functional relationships is much more likely to accept a centralized PMO than a company that has a great deal of internal competition between the functions or has significant friction between leaders. One of the biggest battles a new PMO faces is prioritizing and resourcing projects when there are multiple functions already controlling these projects, specifically "pet" projects, that are of special interest to certain function heads or focused solely on a specific region, but have little prospect of success in the long run.

Before a PMO can be centralized, there first needs to be an assessment of where the project managers currently exist in the organization, how many are there, what functions are they performing, how many projects do they work on and what consistent processes do (or do not) exist currently?

Project Managers typically fall into one of two categories; first the supporting role – where the Project Manager supports a defined team leader. This Project Manager will typically own the timeline, scope, project plan, risk assessment, documentation and send out communications. The second type of Project Manager, my preferred model in a centralized

PMO, is where the Project Manager is the Project Leader, and all team members leave their titles at the conference room door before the meeting begins.

This model requires core team members to suspend their common understanding of the hierarchal structure and see themselves in an execution role for their specific function. The Project Manager as Leader is accountable for the execution, delegation, follow up, communication, escalation, reporting and direction of the activities of the team, with the core team members accountable for their functional deliverables. The team speaks with one voice and reports deliverables, metrics (measurements) and updates as a team. Ideally, these team members have aligned goals and shared metrics to support incentive based performance outcomes. More about metrics in Chapter 7.

In larger companies, where a stake in the performance measures equals a percentage of bonus dollars awarded, if these goals aren't aligned among the team members, then you typically will not have the team members working in harmony to get to the project team goals. Why would they? If I work in Marketing and know I will get my bonus regardless of how well my team does or does not do towards my project deliverables, why would I put myself out? Conversely, if I am the Project Manager and know that my bonus is tied to the execution of my team's deliverables, I'm going to work hard to meet those goals, but I will be disheartened if I miss them and I am penalized, especially if my fellow team members are not. So, there is a strong argument to align project goals, track metrics and report deliverables as a team. To achieve this, you must work with your Human Resources partner and make sure this activity to develop common goals takes place at the right time of the year, when the annual goals definition process gets underway. This is another area where your high-level PMO champion comes into play, as he/she must get the buy-in from other executive function heads to make this work. Unless agreement for aligned goals comes from the top of the organization and is supported by Human Resources processes, there will be significant difficulty in gaining team support for this process.

CHAPTER 2

PROJECT MANAGERS – PEOPLE FIRST

L et's say you get that key agreement to create and centralize a Program Management Office. Congratulations! Now the real work begins – and you have to deliver on what you promised a PMO will do for the company.

Depending on the size of the company you are working in, very likely there are Project Managers working in various departments, who are all now suddenly thrust into new reporting structures as the centralization is announced and implementation begins. Some Project Managers will be happy about that and others will not. In some cases, these may have been very cushy roles where no one was really watching them closely and in other cases, you will have Project Managers that are absolutely yearning to be part of a bigger group that truly has some processes and procedures in place and follows specific project management methodology. One thing you can count on for sure, there will be very different skill sets in the group!

In a previous PMO leadership role, we started with 60 Project Managers tossed together from various functions where they resided, and grew to over 225 Project Managers in the group just 4 years later. While that's a terrific statement of credibility, to achieve that level of growth, the work involved early on to bring these Project Managers together as a team, in advance of proving what an objective PMO could achieve, was a significant effort.

This chapter clearly says, "People First", and the reason is simple; you can have the best processes and procedures anyone has ever imagined, but if you don't have the right people behind you supporting these efforts, you are wasting your time. If your Project Managers don't support you, do not see your support for them, or do not agree with your Vision for the PMO, you just can't expect that you are going to deliver what you promised.

As a leader, you need to know your team, and you are likely looking to select your direct reporting staff as well. It is key to find and select those individuals who believe in your Vision, and are willing to work hard to make it reality. Spending time with the Project Managers, finding out what work they do today (Project Manager in supporting role or Project Manager as Leader), what level of training they have, what their aspirations are and how committed they are to a centralized PMO, is step one of the entire process.

You will quickly learn that there are Project Managers who became Project Managers by osmosis. By that I mean they were simply placed into a Project Manager role because a) they are an organized individual or b) their manager didn't have a role for them and pushed them into a Project Manager position as a holding pattern role until something better came up. You will also find well trained and well-versed Project Managers, hired by functions that knew what they were looking for and hired the appropriate skill set to get the job done.

A quick word about the different Project Management certifications – I have been through all the PMP training courses, 10 or 11 of them if I recall correctly, but I did not sit for the exam, as I had no need to since I was already in a leadership role. The training was great, having followed the PMBOK methodology and outlining all the tools. However, I have never required PMP certification of my Project Management staff. Why? Because I've worked with some terrific Project Managers who did not have this certification, and I've worked with some really inferior Project Managers who did have it. In the nature versus nurture argument, there is something to be said for the fact that great Project Managers definitely have an inherent organizational capability that probably became evident when they were very young, but I do not discount that the ability to organize and project manage is a skill that can be learned. But if it is part of who you are inherently, likely being a Project Manager is much more logical and enjoyable for you to do on a daily basis.

The other question I often receive about certifications is in reference to the Six Sigma Green and Black Belt certifications. Again, this is not a certification I have ever required for Project Manager roles, with the exception of very process driven initiatives that I was accountable for. I have a Six Sigma Black Belt, I'm glad I went through that training because it gave me a very different perspective on projects. As a new project is put in front of me, I look at it from two perspectives, both project structure and process outcome. If it is truly a process driven initiative, then I highly recommend the Black Belt for the role, because it is about improvement and measurement and making sure that the new process meets the expectations. Green Belt training is for anyone, an excellent training that gives you the baseline of what tools a Black Belt utilizes and how to understand them, plus solid reminders of team interactions and working norms that is beneficial to all projects and project teams. If you do find yourself interested in Six Sigma Black Belt training, be sure you are good with, and understand, statistics, as this is a key success factor for taking this training.

Back to your team discussions, it is possible that you will find you have a few tough conversations and decisions as a result of meeting all of your new team members. There will simply be people who should not be in the Project Manager role who somehow landed there years ago. I can recall speaking to a 10-year veteran Project Manager who didn't know how to use Microsoft Project and had no idea what a risk register was, and honestly, didn't enjoy the role and was just collecting a paycheck. If these are good employees, there are always roles for them in the greater organization, and you should try, working with your Human Resources partner, to get them placed elsewhere. But ultimately, you can't keep them in a new and centralized PMO. You are not doing them, or yourself, any favors by keeping them in a role where they cannot perform well and do not want to work anyway. When you hear the saying "you are as strong as your weakest link", it's very true in this situation – because all it takes is one function complaining about their project management support to start to put dents into your PMO's credibility. Placing the right people in the roles is more critical to success than introducing the right tools and processes.

How do you show the new Project Management group that you are working for them as much as you need them working to support you and the projects? Start with what matters most to them; career pathing, job descriptions, training and development.

Defining a career path and consolidating job descriptions go hand in hand. By centralizing a Program Management Office, you are automatically creating a career path that didn't exist previously. When Project Managers exist in the functional organizations, they are outliers. For example, if there are Project Managers in the R&D organization, or in Marketing, they don't fit there and the function seldom creates a career ladder for this role. The Project Manager usually does not have a next step in these functional organizations, because they are placed there as a supporting role, not a core role. A core role in Marketing would be a Product Manager, who would then progress to a Senior Product Manager, to Director of a Product Platform, etc. Whereas the Project Manager would have nowhere to move to other than to wait for the next project to be handed to them. The same would be true for R&D or for Regulatory Affairs, Manufacturing or Finance.

When a PMO is centralized, the job descriptions must be aligned and consolidated to create the career path within the PMO. As an example, when the first 60 Project Managers came together, we pulled all the existing job descriptions for each individual, and found there were approximately 30 different Project Manager job descriptions in total. We took all of these job descriptions and distilled them down to six job descriptions, each with varying degrees of accountability, expectations, and leadership responsibilities. As a group, these six job descriptions formed the career ladder in the PMO. These job descriptions included:

Entry Level Project Support I: Learning the Project Management roles and methodologies, supporting a Project Manager with development of communications, input into a project plan, working on meeting minutes and action item logs.

Project Level Support II: Ready to work on lower level, less complex projects, an example being a small sustaining (product on market) project. Working with a small team with well defined, achievable milestones and deadlines. Supported and mentored by a Project Manager.

Project Manager: Ready to own a project, ready to lead a small team, having proven the ability to meet milestones and deadlines, motivate core team members, negotiate, allocate resources and confront issues successfully. Ready to have one or two direct reports or a potential mentoring relationship with an assigned lower level project support team member.

Senior Project Manager: Ready to lead larger scale projects and have multiple direct reports. Able to lead cross functional teams, escalate issues, present to senior management and be held accountable for results. Responsible for management of the overall project budget.

Program Level Director: Leads a full-scale product development program or Sustaining Projects group. Significant senior management communications and presentations. Full accountability for budget, planning and milestone hit rates within the defined program or product platform. Develops and leads Project Managers and Senior Project Managers.

Senior Director: Leads the program platforms or high value projects in a business unit area and likely sits on the cross functional Business Unit leadership team as well. Accountability for program/project outcomes, reporting, budget alignment and decisions and recommendations regarding project viability.

Years of experience will vary within the above job descriptions, as well as education expectations.

Given that there were thirty different original job descriptions from which the above final six job descriptions were derived, there were subsequent leveling discussions that had to take place with employees. In some cases, individuals received the higher level that corresponded more closely to the work they were doing and the project they were assigned. In other cases, a few employees were de-leveled to a lower job description if the work and the project were defined more closely to that lower level. In the end it balanced out well, with just a few individuals unhappy with where they ended up, but this provided a clear path forward for what they needed to do to regain the next level, which all of them ultimately did within the next 12 to 18 months.

What I did not want these job descriptions to become was a check box exercise, where an employee could go through the job description requirements and check them off and then go to their manager and say "look, I'm at the next level, promote me". So the wording after the requirements indicated that "At the managers discretion, XX years of experience in XX is required". There were also notations that global cross-functional experience was desirable, or that experience managing a group of direct reports for a specific period of time was necessary. I wanted to give the hiring manager the flexibility to manage the leadership expectations that were needed, and to find that right level of executive presence that is always so hard to measure and confirm.

From there, the career path is quite clear, and the progression through the levels well defined. The other key benefit to the centralized PMO, especially in the event where the Project Manager is supporting various business areas, is that there is now the ability to move the Project Managers across the business units, giving them both flexibility to learn new technology areas, and the greater relief of not being out of a job when a project completes. Always knowing there is additional project work in other areas of the PMO is a safety net that helps the Project Managers feel that job security which is vital to getting good results, rather than worrying about what is going to happen when your product is completed and launched.

The individuals in the Senior Director roles are typically the direct reports to the leader of the PMO. These roles walk a very thin line of both accountability to the PMO and managing the relationship and project outcomes with their Business Unit (Marketing) heads. Their role is basically split, with a great deal of responsibility to the projects and project results, and an equal amount of responsibility to their organization and direct reports. These roles require dedication, commitment and complete awareness of all the projects/project issues going on within their teams. The role will typically also push new procedures into the teams as well as monitor existing processes for continuity. The Senior Director role has to be adept at working at the partnerships necessary to create an open environment, where it's safe to have the tough project discussions. Only through the early building of relationships with their business partners, and soliciting ongoing feedback, are they able to achieve success with this dual accountability.

Training

The next area to align for the Project Management Team was their training plans. Not just Project Management training however. How many of you work for larger companies where there are defined training modules that are required on an annual basis? In that first group of 60 Project Managers who we pulled together to form the centralized PMO, there was anywhere from 15 required courses to over 130 required courses per individual. How could there be such a difference? Easy. Because the Project Managers existed in multiple functional areas, they were assigned training modules consistent with or required by that specific functional area. If it was a longer-term employee who had transferred departments a few times over the years, their required courses just transferred with them from the former departments as well – with no one ever paying enough attention to go through and update the required training plans.

This was a time-consuming effort, but well worth the time and much appreciated by the Project Managers. The first step was to identify what training modules were actually required by the PMO and by corporate policy. Utilizing the six new job descriptions, we aligned the training by these job descriptions, matching up the training required based on the expectations of the Project Management role and level.

There are always exceptions. For example, one Business Unit had specific training that was required for anyone, any role, working with their unique products. Any Project Manager supporting that specific Business Unit was required to have those mandatory training modules assigned to their annual training plan.

Ultimately, we reduced the average number of training modules, per Project Manager job description, down to 20-25 training modules. The productivity improvement alone was amazing. For the Project Manager who went from 130+ training modules down to 25 training modules, we likely gave them back 2 to 3 weeks' worth of working productivity effort for their projects.

The benefit of this work went far beyond productivity. The Project Managers were very grateful that the PMO leadership team took the time to review each and every one of their training plans, aligned them to their new job descriptions and then communicated to them what their new plan was. It was simply the attention provided, the fairness and consistency of the process, the effort showing that this was important to us as a new PMO, and to know that every Project Manager had an updated (and relevant) training plan, which bought us a great deal of goodwill from the Project Managers. Note also that it is just as important to annually review this training plan with each employee as part of your goal setting discussions.

After addressing the compulsory corporate training, now it was time to look inward, at our own PMO tools and training. What were our core processes going to be and what training would we offer to our own Project Managers? First, we had to find out what was needed and where our baseline was to start from. As I noted, Project Managers being pulled together for the first time are going to have varying degrees of skills and training and will have been exposed to multiple, likely inconsistent, processes.

I decided that a Skills and Competencies Assessment would be a good starting point to get a handle on where the Project Managers felt they had strong project management skills and where they felt they could use support. The assessment was set up so that each project manager assessed their own areas of skills and competencies with a rating, and then their managers simultaneously rated each Project Manager with their own assessment of their skills and competencies based on their experience with them thus far. The manager did not see the employee's self-assessment prior to doing their own assessment of the employee.

The logistics of the assessment included setting up the questions on a survey monkey like program. The first page of the questionnaire asked the individual for their name, their location, their level (job description), and any certifications that they had related to Project Management (PMP, Six Sigma, other). Keep in mind that participation on this activity was not voluntary – this was a mandatory exercise that all PMO members were expected to complete. With the express intention of providing information regarding what training may or may not be needed, and to facilitate a solid developmental discussion with their manager at mid-year performance review time, there was little resistance to participating.

The competencies that were measured were first grouped into categories – which included:

- Core/Foundational Leadership Skills
- Organization Skills
- Project Management Tools and Process Utilization
- Education, Experience and Technical Skills

Under each of the above categories, there were 5-7 specific questions that team members were asked to rate themselves on a scale of 1-7, with 1 being low and 7 being expert. As a leadership team, prior to the initiation of the assessment, we established a baseline of where we expected each job description level to be at for each skill – and this proved very helpful when seeing the aggregated responses.

When both assessments were completed, the data was then compiled and included where the employee assessed themselves for each item and where the manager assessed the employee on each item. It also included any potential gap that existed between the two ratings. This gap between the ratings, was used to facilitate the conversation between the employee and manager about why the gap existed, why they each rated that skill or competency where they did, and what training or experience could be added to the employee's development plan to address the identified need.

These resulted in a few difficult conversations, especially in light of the fact that in many cases, these were new reporting situations and the employee and manager had not really come together yet to form a trusting relationship. In hindsight, I would have waited longer to perform this action, since the trust wasn't yet there and there was a rumored concern that we were looking to remove the less skilled Project Managers from their roles as we were forming the centralized PMO. While we did identify areas of initial training that was needed, we were much more successful two years later when we followed up this assessment once the manager/employee relationships were stronger and the activities of the centralized PMO well defined, proven and accepted.

As I had learned from other companies, when you have a PMO that has an international component, there are cultural norms that need to be taken into consideration, especially when asking individuals to rate themselves or when asking them what training they need. Europeans, in my experience, will request training, training, training, even for items they have been trained in multiple times. Additionally, I had learned that in certain parts of Europe, it is considered arrogant or rude to rate yourself highly in self assessments, and we saw that very quickly in the gap results from the skills and competencies assessment work. Strong and confident Project Managers rated themselves exceptionally low in many areas, and we simply had to exclude those results once we realized it was an entire location that rated themselves that poorly.

Following the assessment, the aggregation, the comparison with the manager's results and the one on one meetings to review the results with each employee, we followed up with a survey (completely anonymous) to ask what went well with the process and what did not. The results were overwhelmingly positive and comments cited the open and candid discussions that the employees had with their manager and the ability to create meaningful development and training plans.

We now had the initial information we needed to find out what kinds of processes were already in place and where the Project Managers needed support. With this information, we were able to develop a training plan that would align to the roll out of the new processes, yet to be introduced or implemented, that would be the first foray into the improvement of our project metrics, and the first step to prove that a centralized PMO would be of value to the company.

Other Project Management Support Tools

With the development of a centralized PMO, communications become a critical element of the day to day working structure. Not the project work, which we will discuss in later chapters, but the elements of support so necessary to a working PMO.

As a leader, I wanted to put in place multiple support tools to assist, but there also needed to be that personal interaction on a regular basis that was required as a visible attribute of support. Below are some of the items that worked well in previous companies, that were carried over many times in my leadership roles:

- One on One meetings with my direct reports. Starting on a weekly basis and moving to bi-weekly meetings at the end of one year, this helped me to get to know the person, the projects and the challenges that were being faced by the leadership team (direct reports). Often this included getting bottom up information separately from the teams themselves, and learning where the rough patches were in the organization from discussions with Project Managers or other core team members from other functions. This allowed me to provide individual feedback to my leadership team members as well as run interference in any areas that were escalated to me for attention. Development needs were always addressed during these conversations as well. To help build trust, I would always ask for feedback on my own activities too. Were there too many new processes and procedures being rolled out at once? Was I paying enough attention to their concerns or was I being pulled to too many other issues corporately and not engaged enough? These had to be "safe" conversations, and if something was asked to be kept private (with the exception of something that had to be reported from an HR or patient safety perspective), it would always be kept confidential.
- Skip Level Meetings were held twice per year. This was a one on one meeting with the direct reporting staff members to my leadership team. This was an opportunity for me to interact closely with individuals that were the next level within the organization and often communicated to by my leadership team rather than by me directly. These were more structured meetings, with me preparing my own agenda to ask specific questions about their programs, teams, and their individual concerns. It always surprised me that there were usually one or two follow ups from these meetings, which I paid close attention to keeping up my end of any follow up required. If there was a perception that I was holding these meetings just for show, there would quickly be little value derived from them going forward.

- Focus Groups were held monthly, and did not include anyone at the director level and up. My admin would randomly select 10-12 PMO team members to join me for a one-hour coffee chat, which had no identified agenda and was open to all questions and issues. There were always some items that were rumors and could not be addressed, and that was understood, but if there was information that could be provided, I openly discussed it with the attendees. These meetings were only ever held in person. No teleconference or WebEx was used and that was done purposely so that the interactions were face to face. When I traveled overseas to our other locations, then multiple focus groups were held at those locations to keep the momentum going at those international locations as well. Special effort was given to mix up the attendees and to include members from different teams that supported various Business Units. There were focus groups where introductions were actually necessary because the Project Managers had not met each other previously or had worked in other areas where they had not had the ability to have interactions with other team members. The best way to know if these are successful meetings is when someone can't make it due to vacation or business travel, they specifically ask to be re-scheduled so they can attend the next available session. When that happens, you know that these focus groups are valued and considered worth the employees' time.
- Town Hall Meetings were held quarterly and included the entire membership of the PMO, regardless of location or time zone. There were times when audio or video challenges made it so difficult that we had to hold separate sessions for the international team, but this was rare. When it did happen, it would soon be apparent that it worked better this way, to hold the international session separately, because they felt disenfranchised on the phone, did not understand the private jokes that were mentioned during the meeting, or just felt left out overall, like spectators to a party they should have been part of. Town Hall meetings were an opportunity to announce organization changes, highlight successes, process or procedure changes, budget planning expectations, new tools or

training opportunities. Since the PMO had so many diverse projects underway, we sometimes used this as an opportunity to update the entire team on the actions of a specific team and their success. Individual recognition was always a welcome discussion topic as well as team accomplishments. Special guests, whether senior leaders from other functions or guest speakers talking about project management issues, were additional topics we included when available. By far however, the most interesting presentations and talks came from patients who were utilizing the products that we worked on. In the years where I worked for either pharmaceutical or medical device companies, nothing compared to hearing from the patients that could talk about the impact that our work had on their lives on a daily basis. That's when our work hit home and when we really understood why we put in the extra hours and chased our deadlines as closely as we did. The work we did truly made a difference in the day to day quality of life for these individuals.

- PMO Monthly Training Sessions were offered to all team members. These were not mandatory sessions, but always of interest. On a quarterly basis, at least one session would include Lessons Learned from a recently completed project. This was identified in an internal audit as a requirement for us, to hold regularly scheduled Lessons Learned briefings. Other topics would include "101" sessions, learning about the Regulatory Affairs or the Global Pharmacovigilance organization and processes. Occasionally, we would introduce new project management tools, or tips and hints of how to utilize existing tools properly.

- A PMO Handbook was developed by a volunteer team of Project Managers and kept up to date on a twice-yearly basis. The handbook was split into two sections, the first being very employee driven items, including how to do expense vouchers, how to order stationery, purchase orders and requisitions, and many other onboarding type items. The second half of the handbook was very specific to the PMO processes, including full explanations, links and who to contact for additional information and/or training. This second section included topics such as the product development process, resource allocation, milestone management, project governance and contracts, and essentially all of the processes that the Project Manager was expected to be utilizing in their role. The PMO handbook became a standard which was copied by many other organizations in the company.

- The PMO Buddy System was introduced to help with our on-going integrations and acquisitions. The buddy system process became another standard which other functions quickly adopted and utilized. When the buddy system was first introduced within the PMO, it was expressly to help with onboarding new hires. A newly hired Project Manager was paired with an existing Project Management employee, to be the individual that a) takes them to lunch on day one and makes introductions to others into the organization, b) checks in with the new employee on a regular basis along with showing the new hire where the tools are located for the PMO members, and c) is the individual that the new PMO employee can go to with the questions that they do not want to ask their new manager. This relationship typically lasts about six to eight weeks, until the new hire (or new transfer from another part of the company) is fully comfortable with the people, processes, culture and knows where to find the tools to do the job. I also found this Buddy System to be extremely useful during mergers and acquisitions, where we had to onboard employees into the organization from other companies, regardless of location (which in some cases was international). Buddies were assigned to Project Managers in multiple international sites, with a six-week expectation that for one hour each week, the buddies would talk and share information, tools, tips, procedures and just get to know the individual so that the newly acquired Project Managers had their first friend and contact in the PMO organization. Incredibly successful, the buddies often stayed in touch on a regular basis, well beyond the six-week program expectation, and during business travel made it a point to meet up in person when business travel took them to the location where the buddy was located. There was a follow-up survey completed at the completion of the international buddy system program, and there was a 90% positive response rate to the program. After sharing the results of this survey with senior leaders, other functions quickly took up the activity with the same excellent results overall.

- A PMO SharePoint site was developed just for the PMO team members. Items placed here included an acronym listing, checklists, such as how to transfer, hold or terminate a project, lessons learned, various sample templates, project management articles of interest, training information, Town Hall decks, Human Resources presentations to the team, the PMO handbook, and a link to "ask Karen" (which was a Q&A text box where anyone could ask me a question and everyone would see both the question and the response). Additionally, all training materials for the PMO, job descriptions, and templates and samples for our tools and processes were located on this site.

- A separate Onboarding site was pulled together for the new Project Management hires, transfers and acquired employees. Included on this site was a video introduction from me welcoming them into the organization, talking through the PMO Vision, and then explaining what information the onboarding site would provide to them. The video was a guided tour of all the tools available on the site to assist them with performing the Project Management role. From first explaining the expectations of the Buddy System, to explaining the role of the PMO within the broader organization, to details of what they could expect from a communications perspective and ending with my expectations of them in their new project management role, these new PMO team members were welcomed and quickly made aware of the numerous resources available to them that only a centralized PMO model can provide.

- Twice Annually New Hire Meeting. This meeting was held so that I had an opportunity to meet the new hires/transfers into the PMO organization on a regular basis. Any new PMO team member hired within the last six months was asked to attend. Similar to the Focus Groups explained earlier, there was no specific agenda, each new hire/transfer was asked to introduce themselves, their background, their expectations in joining the PMO, followed by my personal introduction and expectations for their role. This was my opportunity to make sure that I met and knew every individual in the PMO and that they had an opportunity to provide me with their first impressions. I was specifically interested in listening to confirm that each new hire/transfer had an assigned buddy, knew where to find the PMO resources, and knew who to reach out to if they were not getting consistent onboarding attention. In holding this meeting, it truly confirmed that each PMO new hire/transfer was being given that level of attention, since the managers were all aware that this meeting was always scheduled and they didn't want to be the one called out for not having their new hires being properly onboarded. It would be very clear in that meeting who was receiving strong onboarding and orientation to the PMO and who was not receiving any onboarding support.

- Fun Events. Whether the PMO has a large number of team members or is a small group, you need to make the time to schedule some fun events as a team. When coming together in a centralized model, this is even more important since these individuals more than likely have not met before. If you want them to interact as a team, they need to know each other, feel comfortable with each other and share the same desire to prove what a centralized PMO model can do for the company. Definitely less formal that actual teambuilding exercises, but I found that these events were often more successful in developing relationships. Some of the events held included a Chili Cook Off Contest, where participants brought in crock pots of their own special chili recipes, which were then taste tested and voted upon. We had little Chili Pot trophies for the awards. Pot Luck events for the sake of just getting together, and of course, the annual Christmas Pot Luck luncheon. In a recent role, this Christmas luncheon also included a gift exchange called a White Elephant. I was unfamiliar with the term, but essentially everyone brought in a $10 gift, and not necessarily a nice gift, perhaps something that has been in the garage and didn't sell at a yard sale comes to mind, and some nicer gifts as well. After drawing numbers, individuals go in order to select and open a gift. If they don't like their gift, they can take a gift from anyone who has already opened their gift previously. So as you can imagine, the worst gifts get passed around pretty quickly, while the nicer gifts are coveted and also change hands often. Other potential opportunities to build our team included special volunteer events, such as Habitat for Humanity, where teams would help build homes for the day, or a half day volunteering as a team at a local food bank. Pictures of these events were always posted on the PMO SharePoint site and included in Newsletters or other recognition type distributions.

- And speaking of recognition, this is an opportunity area not to be overlooked. Not just for the Project Managers, but for the teams themselves, who work so hard to meet the milestones, expectations and goals of their projects. In the various companies I worked for, I've seen multiple methods. The first method was in a Big Pharma model, where there was a set dollar amount that was distributed after product launch, along with a crystal memento or some other commemorative item. In this specific company, the award amount was differentiated by Core Team Member versus Extended Team Member. What was nice about it was that everyone received something, and specifically with Pharma projects, which can take many years to complete, a listing was kept of all individuals who worked on the team over the years, and seldom was anyone left out, regardless of the time lapse since they had worked on the project. Many companies also hold award events for projects that exceed the stated goals of the project. These are usually evening events with a dinner, gift and monetary or stock token of appreciation. What I was fortunate enough to do in one company was to hold specific Project Management Awards, recognizing a Project Manager of the Year and a Project Team of the Year. This event was held during working hours, had a guest speaker, either an internal senior leader or an external speaker, followed by photos with the winders and a networking reception. While initially well received, after a few years support waned and projects were not being submitted for nomination in the numbers we had previously seen. This, coupled with financial cut backs, ended the program. The bottom line is that Project Managers should always be conscious of recognition opportunities for their deserving teams. Teams that exceed their milestones and goals, should always be recognized for their exceptional efforts. It's important to also recognize the cancelled or failed project. When a project is cancelled by the business, more than likely a great deal of work has been done thus far, and its difficult work to close a project mid-stream. These projects deserve recognition too – the amount of money saved by making a solid decision to end a project that has zero prospects, for whatever reason, is ultimately a valuable opportunity to recognize the individuals who worked on the activity.

CHAPTER 3

Relationships/Stakeholders

A key element to a successful PMO is the relationships you build with the stakeholders and those you will be supporting. In the case of a newly centralized PMO, negotiate with your boss the time it will take to meet with the key stakeholders in advance of starting to implement new tools, procedures or processes.

Before I go fully into this topic, keep in mind that a PMO is a cyclical organization. By that I mean that a PMO can be centralized, then decentralized, then centralized again – usually with a 3-5-year lifecycle. I've seen this happen more times than I can count, and in multiple companies. Why does this happen? A few reasons:

1. A new leader at the top of an organization. They may have a very different mindset than the previous leader and prefer one model over the other (centralized versus decentralized) for not just PMO, but for all parts of the company they are leading.

2. After a few years in a centralized model, things are running well, projects are achieving consistent milestones and stage gates, and generally all status and portfolio information is on target and being distributed on a regular basis. When things start to run this smoothly, what usually happens is that there is a belief that the centralized PMO is not needed, because there is little recognition that this is the organization keeping the wheels on the bus to begin with. PMO is always a target opportunity area to reduce

costs. Like most "service" functions in any large organization, these functions are always the first targets for cost reductions.

3. Weakness or inconsistency with project support. If the perception exists that not all Project Managers are following the same guidelines or tools, or that some Project Managers do not have the right skill sets for certain projects, there tends to be a bit of a revolt by other functions that do not believe they are getting the best Project Managers assigned to their projects. This is very prevalent at the beginning of a centralized model, where you need to weed through which Project Managers are truly skilled and which ones may have just been placed into Project Manager roles to save their job. Additionally, in large companies with more family orientated cultures, the protectionism that can take place is something to be reckoned with. Not only will some managers protect individuals who are honestly not capable of performing the Project Manager role, the team will protect the individual as well. Going as far as covering for individuals who are incapable of performing the work (any function), to protect the job of that employee. This is a cultural issue, which becomes harder to address the larger the PMO becomes, since it then becomes easier for the leaders to cover for the less skilled Project Managers.

4. A belief that the PMO belongs under R&D. Sometimes this is just ambitious R&D leaders who want to empire build, but why anyone believes that a PMO belongs solely under R&D is beyond my comprehension. Placing Project Managers under R&D could potentially ruin the opportunity to have Project Managers run any project that is not a New Product Development of Sustaining/Maintenance type project. There are so many other projects within the overall company that a centralized PMO could be leading. This would include Innovation activities such as University partnerships and / or 3rd party development opportunities, initiative level projects like merger and acquisition support, etc., and then functional level projects, where the PMO is lent out to support other functions with their specific initiatives. Secondly, and most importantly, if the PMO

exists under R&D, no matter what effort you may put into placing the PMO into a position of objectivity, it simply doesn't hold water. Every other function will automatically assume that the PMO will do as R&D dictates, since that's where they are paid from. Losing the ability to have that perceived level of objectivity infused into the PMO organization is an absolute predictor of failure and/or certain decentralization in the 3 to 5-year PMO lifecycle.

Even if the new PMO is becoming centralized for a second or third time, take the opportunity to meet with the existing stakeholders to find out what worked well in the past, what didn't work, and most importantly, what their expectations are for the PMO. Especially in cases where the PMO is being resurrected, there will be lessons to be learned about why the centralized model failed in the past, or even just the perception of why it failed previously.

The larger element to this conversation should focus on getting critical buy-in to your new ideas too. This is your opportunity to meet your stakeholders one on one, tell them individually what tools and processes you are planning to implement, all to get their buy-in, well in advance of your roll out of these activities or initiatives. The importance of this activity cannot be underestimated. Without this advance buy-in, you risk the rejection of your plans, or worse, the unwillingness for the stakeholder to have their function support your plans.

When people feel heard, you get their support. You are giving the stakeholder the ability to be heard and to provide you with their ideas about the plans you want to implement. Sometimes, that's all they need – to feel as if they had a say in what you are about to do, had a chance to pre-approve your ideas and contribute to them. Additionally, with stakeholders who have been with the company long term, you get valuable insights into what has or has not worked well in the past, and sometimes a bit more perspective about some of the more difficult stakeholders you are about to meet with. With a little luck, and good negotiation skills, your ideal outcome is for one stakeholder to smooth the path with another, more difficult stakeholder, for you. After all, what they want to really know is what is in it for them? What do your ideas bring to the table that will advance their project or their specific agenda?

Take the time to think through these conversations in advance of holding them. Know your audience, know their role and what you would want a PMO to do for you if you were sitting in that position. Even if you are new to the company, learn about your stakeholder's function and the key projects for their area of responsibility.

This does take time away from your implementation activities, but it is time well spent because your implementations will go much smoother in the long run. As noted previously, if you already have the support of a strong executive sponsor of the PMO, perhaps this is the individual who hired you into this leadership role, to have that individual make these stakeholder introductions for you is incredibly valuable to start these relationships off on the right foot.

The relationship with the stakeholder doesn't stop here, and it is a relationship that needs to be tended to on a regular basis. Ask each stakeholder during your first discussion how often they want you to keep them updated, and do they prefer this update to be in person, by phone or by email? Give them the opportunity to define the contact interval and what is most important to them from an information perspective. There is no better way to cultivate the relationship and keep that continued support from them, than by letting the stakeholder define what it is they want and expect by way of ongoing contact.

These are meetings that you should make every effort NOT to move or reschedule. Likely these stakeholders are at your level or above, and how you treat these meetings will quickly show them how valuable you perceive the meeting to be.

I recommend not scheduling meetings for the long term, (other than expected monthly interval meetings such as staff meetings), but instead doing a quarterly meeting schedule. This plan includes my one on one meetings with my direct reports as well. As a leader, when you do a lot of shuffling and rescheduling of meetings, and most of the time it is because your boss does exactly the same, forcing the domino effect, it gives the employee or team that you were to meet with a feeling that they are not as important as whatever it is that caused you to move the meeting in the first place. You want to avoid this at all costs, and keep your meeting commitments as much as possible.

CHAPTER 4

EARLY WINS

I f you are new to the company, defining the criteria for early wins will come from multiple sources: Your boss, your stakeholders, your employees, and the company history of metrics (assuming this information exists). Early wins are the low hanging fruit we hear so much about, the quick hits that will rapidly show how valuable the new PMO is. The trick is to select the right items to target.

Following your introductory discussions with your manager, stakeholders and employees, you will likely have a strong indication of where opportunity for improvement exists. Perhaps there is little predictability in milestones, or lack of status updates, zero prioritization, no governance process or lack of understanding project resource requirements. Imagine being faced with all of the above!

This is where company culture comes into the discussion; how much change can the organization take at one time? How willing is your newly formed PMO team to trust and follow your lead skillfully and enthusiastically? How well did you do in creating and forming relationships with your stakeholders and your team members? You need to have confidence in these elements before you roll out your first major procedural change. You should have already invested significant time in the development of the Project Manager elements (Chapter 2) to garner their support, as well as your stakeholder meetings, and just as importantly, connected with someone deep inside the organization who has been with the company for many years, to understand the culture and what level of change you can affect quickly. If the company is large enough to have a Change Management function, this is definitely a target topic with that group. Absent a Change Management function, your best bet is a long term Human Resource professional that supports your organization and knows the ins and outs of the culture and current politics.

Selecting the first target area for your initial implementation should encompass something that touches all your stakeholders and is important to the company performance metrics, essentially a large enough impact to provide both credibility for the PMO and for you as a leader.

In a previous role, new to the organization, I was pretty shocked to see that the milestone achievement rate for the projects, for the entire year, was a staggering 50%. Without truly looking at what those milestones were, how well thought out they were, whether they were honestly milestones or just simple activities, this clearly became a quick win target area to address, and was the first item selected for implementation.

In a decentralized PMO model, clearly there were no guidelines surrounding what milestones were used, if leading indicators were considered or strictly stage gates included, or how the milestones were being collected and tracked. Ultimately, how the planning of the milestones was performed was also at issue. But one thing was very clear from sitting in multiple team meetings, missed milestones were happening at the last minute and were "surprising" when they were missed.

If you work in the Project Management field, you already know that this had to be false. If a team will miss a major project milestone, more than 90% of the time the team knows this many weeks in advance of that expected milestone date. But here it was all happening last minute. What does that tell you? It says that team members were afraid to escalate, if there was even a prescribed escalation path available, and that no one was willing to step up and say there was a problem to senior management until it was essentially too late to do anything about it. What a perfect area for an early win!

In the Project Management world, we are told every project should have a Project Charter. I don't really like Project Charters at all. They're fine at the start of a project when you outline what is expected or needed for the project result, but how many times can you say that you've seen the Project Charter updated on a regular basis? It's a lot of work up front that gets lost or ignored down the road. I am far more a fan of a Project Contract instead.

A Project Contract can be a valuable tool throughout the lifecycle of the new product development project. If done correctly, the Project Contract becomes the agreement, within stage/phase, between the project team and the governance team. The Project Contract states what the team will achieve in that specific phase, with tolerances around each area. Once the Project Contract is accepted by the governance team, the assumption is that what was agreed to will be achieved, and if it is not, it is an automatic trigger for that project team to return to the governance team to review the project and re-align the Project Contract dates and milestones accordingly.

Implementing the Project Contract gave permission for projects to ask for help. As opposed to hiding the issues until the last minute when nothing could be done about them, having the Project Contract laid the expectation that the team could and should escalate issues early, whether the issues were financial or resource related, it was permission for the team to get the attention that they needed, without the prospect of punishment. It was the contractual expectation between the Project Team and the governance committee of what would be achieved, and the promise of support from the governance committee to help out if they needed to by providing additional finances or resources, if escalation occurred.

A Project Contract contains a good amount of information about the project. This includes the scope, the timeline to launch, where the launches will take place (the wave of launches), the expected pricing, planned revenue expectations, key challenges and who the team members are on the project. Usually just three to four pages long, the Project Contract encompasses those key elements and deliverables that a team plans to achieve within a specific product development phase such as Concept, Feasibility, Development, Verification and Validation or Launch. If the Project Contract is going to be utilized, there needs to be an integration of the actual Project Contract tool into the existing Product Development Process within the company. Keeping in mind your stakeholder process – the Product Development Process Owner will need to agree to add this tool into the process going forward.

Earlier I mentioned the tolerances in the Project Contract. These tolerances, or variances as you may want to refer to them, are plus/minus amounts on the various deliverables. For example, if the timeline for the stage gate review is February 15th, and you are in the Feasibility Phase, I would add a plus minus of 8 weeks to that date. Therefore, as long as the stage gate is completed between January 15th and March 15th, the Project Contract for this specific item is intact and has not been breached. Depending on which stage/phase the project is in, the tolerances will become looser or tighter. The earlier the project phase, the looser the tolerance needs to be. The later the phase of the project, when the expectations and known issues are far more fleshed out, then the allowed tolerances should be much tighter since the risks should be well known. As always, this varies by project, so I was never inclined to provide absolute guidance on what the plus/minus targets were to be. Every project is different, and what works for one will not, and should not, work for another. Product Development Projects are not one size fits all projects. If they were, we wouldn't need Project Managers. The recommendation was that the team work out the individual tolerances for their Project Contracts, review with the PMO Leaders and then present to the Governance Committee for acceptance.

Once a Contract was accepted, the team was to proceed with their work, and only return to the Governance Committee for one of 2 reasons; a) the contract was breached and the team needed support/resources or b) the team completed that phase and they were coming in for a scheduled stage gate review, which automatically would include the presentation of the next stage's Project Contract for agreement.

The only other reasons why a Project Team would be called in off schedule to a Governance Committee meeting would be in the event of significant technology changes in the marketplace, competitor issues or legal concerns, or a business level decision to shut down the project, possibly for cost reasons.

With the concept of a Project Contract agreed to with all stakeholders, the next step was to introduce the tool to the Project Managers, who ultimately had to introduce it into their teams to get the information to populate the Project Contract. Initially skeptical about the Project

Contract, the Project Managers quickly saw the tool as an opportunity for an escalation path that was clearly missing, and a welcome opportunity to highlight issues as well as showcase achievements of their project teams.

As with each of the implementation areas that were identified, we utilized Pilot Teams to begin the process. With Project Contracts, we selected 3-4 well run and active teams to be our pilots. They worked to fill in the Project Contract, had the Contracts reviewed by PMO leadership and then presented to the business unit leads for their agreements. One month was allotted for the development of the pilot Project Contracts, and the teams we selected were enthusiastic and easily completed the work on time. Choosing the right teams to pilot any of the initiatives was critical, since not all teams are high functioning or have strong Project Management leadership. If the pilot teams selected were not going to fully embrace the process we were introducing, it was a guarantee that when the tool was rolled out to the broader group, there would be little chance of success. The work of the pilot teams was often the roadmap for the later teams to utilize as they prepared their Project Contracts. In the case of the weaker and less engaged teams, this was invaluable to be able to provide them with sample information for them to work from.

A huge part of the acceptance of the Project Contract was the Governance Committee, and for the first time the Project Teams would have access to senior leadership to gain awareness of and support for their projects. It had to go hand in hand that the Project Contracts would roll out along with the implementation of the Governance Committee.

During the pilot phase of the Project Contracts, the Governance Committee was formed. This needed to be a high-level senior team, at the very top levels of the company, with a remit and a commitment to ensure the success of the projects. In a short amount of time, the responsibility for prioritization of the projects would also fall to this Governance Committee as well.

Back to my earlier note about having your executive champion for the PMO -- this is the individual who will also help pull this Governance Committee together and gather support for the process. While you may have already met with many of these leaders as part of your stakeholder meetings, your executive champion likely works at the same peer level with these individuals, and his/her direct involvement in harnessing their compliance is critical to the success of the governance process.

Once defined, the Governance Team had their first meeting, which was mainly about what to expect and what the Project Contract was, what it included and what the expectations of the Project Teams were going to be during the meetings. Meetings were held monthly to start, since there were so many Project Contracts and teams to review, but then moved to quarterly meetings once projects moved into a regular cadence of stage gate reviews. The Governance Committee would also take on another role in the management of projects – Prioritization, and this will be discussed in a later chapter.

Now that we have identified what the first early win will be, and we have the tool, process and pilot teams in place to implement, there was still a need to understand what milestones were being included in the previous process and how could there be assurance that both planning and selection of these milestones had solid consistency in the new model?

First, we had to be sure to include all stage gates as a milestone for any project that had set stage gates during the coming year. Secondly, we needed to protect the launch dates of the projects, regardless of whether or not they planned to be held in the upcoming year, and finally, predictive indicators needed to be added. Predictive indicators were activities, actions or deliverables, that taken alone, and either successfully or unsuccessfully achieved, would indicate whether or not the upcoming milestone noted would or would not be hit. As a simple example, if the supplier was unable to ship the materials by a specific date, then clearly the product would not be available on the planned launch date.

Every project was required to have at least 1 milestone per quarter, and more critical projects may have had as many as one milestone per month. The milestones were tracked by New Product Development projects and Sustaining/Maintenance (on market) products. Additionally, Innovation Projects were also tracked separately. I've also seen the New Product Development products split by pipeline in very large companies. The split is into Early Stage versus Late Stage Development Projects, and this makes good sense in these larger companies with large pipelines, since once a project gets through to the Development Stage, moving it into a separate pipeline with more attentive tracking, ensures that these projects which have full commitment at this point, are even more closely monitored for success than the Early Stage pipeline which has many unknowns at this point in the project lifecycle.

A key learning for our team was to not use specific dates but to instead use the end of the month as the milestone target date, and for large scale projects in the Early Stage, to use the end of the quarter as the key milestone. Not only did this provide a bit more buffer than what the Project Manager may have included, but it also allowed for easier tracking of the milestones, since leaders were always watching for the end of the month or end of the quarter knowing that's when the due dates would fall.   This also provided for easier reporting consistency since reports generated during the first week of the month were always up to date.

It was mainly the international countries that balked at the use of the end of the month or end of the quarter dates, as it appeared that their preference was to call out a specific date for each milestone regardless of where that date fell in the month. It took time, but once there was an understanding of the intent of consistency, they were onboard. And the very first time that the buffer came into play, saving the milestone commitment by 2 weeks instead of missing the milestone completely, there was much more appreciation for the logic behind the use of the end of month or end of quarter timing.

With all the steps in place, the first early win implementation was underway. Project Contracts were prepared in advance of the new year and the new Governance Committee was in place. The end result of the first full year of implementation? A 90% milestone hit rate, which was repeated and improved over a period of 5 years following. A definite great start and the first of many implementations to build the credibility and value of the PMO.

CHAPTER 5

PORTFOLIO MANAGEMENT, PRIORITIZATION & GOVERNANCE

Not all Program Management Offices are fortunate enough to also have a Portfolio function included in their scope and organization. There are pros and cons to both structures yet I tend to believe that there is a strong value in initially having the portfolio team report into the PMO, since they can get closer to the projects and understand the reporting needs. Long term however, I feel that Portfolio Management should reside in a corporate function, so it can support Investor Relations requirements as well as provide the level of response to requests that usually only comes with a corporate reporting structure. Just like the PMO, when Portfolio Management is sitting within other functions, and not in a corporate role, the perception is that the Portfolio Management group will reflect and report what the owning function wants it to, skewing results and reports to their function's best interest instead of the company's best interest. Similar to the PMO, you will want Portfolio Management placed in a position of objectivity, which is usually reporting corporately.

A Portfolio Management group can have multiple responsibilities; management of the pipeline information, ownership of any available resource management tools, participation in the budget planning for the projects and ownership of any portfolio, milestone and metrics tools within the organization. Additionally, the function must have the capability and competency to train on these tools, mentor and support the

Project Managers in their use, plus cajole them into meeting the deadlines for inputs.

As the conduit from Project Management to Investor Relations, the Portfolio Management group is the keeper of the pipeline information, gleaned from the many Project Contracts and updates that are funneled through the PMO. The Investor Relations (IR) needs are usually sudden, with a quick turn-around time required, and normally has to do with tracking launches and revenue expectations out for the number of years as defined in the Long-Range Plan. But once the metrics are defined for the entire PMO plan, the Portfolio Management group will also track and report on those as well.

As an example, let's take the milestone metrics that were part of the early wins topic we just reviewed in the last chapter. The process for the development of these milestones is annual, beginning possibly in October/November, when the Project Managers meet with their teams to review not only their current Project Contracts, but also their plans for the coming year. This includes budget and resource needs as well as expected milestones. The PMO Leads then follow up with their teams to review this information for accuracy and then the Project Manager makes any updates to the Portfolio Management tool (assuming one exists!) following this approval.

The Portfolio Management group takes these milestones from the Portfolio Management tool, and then issues the reports on the status of these milestones on a regular basis. The first reports go out to the PMO Leadership team, who review for accuracy and confirm that the information is as expected from the previous discussion and accurate. The report will not only provide the percentages, updates and changes to the milestones, it will also include a detailed section as to why any milestones were missed or changed. The distribution will include all the stakeholders from the multiple businesses and functions within the company, so accuracy is critical.

This is just one of the many areas where the Portfolio Management group will be active. Their role extends far beyond reporting and well into partnership with the Project Managers, Financial team members, PMO Leads and Functional Heads. While they will work closely with all of these individuals, it is still a garbage in/garbage out situation, and the tools they use and the reports they create, will only be as good as the information they are given and as accurate as the latest data provided to them.

The actual management of the pipeline is the essence of the work of the Portfolio Management group. When the company is large and the pipeline is significant, perhaps broken into multiple pipelines (early stage, late stage, innovation, on market products) or all together, there still comes a point where it is valuable to prioritize the projects. Specifically, for the Shared Services functions, such as Sterility or Stability testing, those functions have no way of knowing which projects needs to be worked on first, and they will often fall back to who is screaming the loudest or has the highest-level individual emailing them to put their project work next into the queue.

Prioritization is valuable not only from the perspective of Shared Services work, but it also takes away the "pet" project protection, since all projects are evaluated objectively in a good prioritization process. I know there are tools devoted to project prioritization, yet in a company that understands their projects and knows their long-term objectives, there should be no reason why project prioritization needs to be a massive effort. The main work is in the initial prioritization effort and in the ongoing management of the pipeline, ensuring that it is not just a once per year exercise to do this prioritization work.

This effort goes hand in hand with the Stage Gate review process, and for projects that are not performing or where technology changes or competitive factors are hindering the ongoing project work, these projects need to also have their priority updated to reflect these changes so that other projects can potentially receive and utilize the resources, both financial and people, that can be moved (skill set permitting) from one project to advance another. In the situation where there is close attention to the pipeline and the prioritization takes place on a regular basis, these attributes are taken into consideration continuously, along with the Project Contract progress, and utilized to update the project prioritization listing.

Step one for prioritization is getting agreement from the Governance Team that this is not a once a year process. For prioritization to be effective, the pipeline and prioritization has to be reviewed on a regular basis and in some cases, very tough decisions need to be made quickly.

Leaving a project in the pipeline while it is floundering for a year is throwing money out the window, as is knowing that a technology that you are feverishly working on has already been outdated or that a competitor has already gone to market with the same or similar product you have in the pipeline. All of these scenarios require quick changes and reallocation of resources, both people and dollars.

Prioritization can be done in many ways, yet taking the time to analyze the best criteria for the company's goals, and aligning the prioritization values to these criteria, is a good methodology to use to start the prioritization process.

Utilizing a weighting factor – with equal weights assigned to each metric, I have previously used the following criteria:

- The rank of the project within the business unit (which assumes multiple business units in the company)
- The level of complexity of the project (which requires assigning a level of complexity to the projects early on)
- Net Present Value of the Project
- Expected sales of the product at the 5-year mark
- The amount of the remaining costs of the project until true launch
- The expected Return on Investment
- Overall Capital expenditure
- Probability of Success ratio

In the event that a tie breaker was needed, additional criteria for consideration included Launch Year or Internal Rate of Return.

The first time this exercise is done is the largest investment in time and training. Assigning the project the weighing and then compiling the outcomes requires dedicated effort for a few weeks, plus creating the reports that interpret the outcomes. The initial outcome is what I called the natural order. Based on the weighting and scoring, the projects fall into a natural order and are easily ranked. But seldom is this order the right order for the company. In fact, most senior leaders get upset when they see the natural order because it does not reflect what is most important to their business. That's a clear indicator that the business cases, where these attributes are first noted and where the weighting is assigned from, are a bit "fluffed". Because if the attributes were accurate, the natural order would be too.

I have noted that no prioritization tool is 100% perfect and that all prioritization tools require some level of logic to be applied. Therefore, once the natural order is available, the Portfolio team would return to the leaders and ask them to look over the order and confirm that the most important projects are in the order they expected to see. As the process progressed over time, this became much easier, but in the beginning the order was never what the business expected. The new logical order was then completed, by business unit, and ultimately combined to the full portfolio across all business units within the company.

The compilation into the full corporate prioritization usually went pretty easily, since the projects were in the logical order by then and senior leadership would quickly slot the projects into the overall priority order, sometimes working within categories to ensure funding was available for all the projects. The budget line was drawn across the project spend for the priority order and it was amazing to see how many projects could not be funded when the budget constraint was added in. These projects that were unfunded were then moved to a buy-up list, and were later moved into the active pipeline as other projects completed or were stopped. But once a project was moved to the buy-up list, all work ceased and all resources were moved to other projects that were active and funded.

Once Prioritization of the projects is established and communicated, the management of the priority list should ideally become part of the same overall Project Governance process, by the same team that approves new ideas into the pipeline and the same team that is the escalation point for Project Contract or Stage Gate issues. This, the highest-level Governance Committee, is the group that needs to have the oversight, ability and commitment to make the tough decisions to keep the pipeline on track to meet the corporate goals and the Investor Relations commitments (assuming a publicly held company).

The Portfolio Management Team should be in attendance during these pipeline discussions, and should have a tool available that provides the ability to model the project pipeline. For example, if there is a decision to place Project B on hold, the tool should be able to quickly show what the impact would be if those resources, both people and financial, were to move to Project D instead. But it is up to the PMO Leadership to caution that moving money or people to other projects does not automatically ensure that a project will move forward any quicker. There are times when no amount of additional financial support will move a project from its current point. Moving people to a new project does not guarantee that the individuals that are being moved have the right skill set to actually assist the project.

The PMO Leadership should not only be facilitating this Governance Committee, they should also take the time to train this group in what to expect, what kind of decisions they will be asked to make, and what tools will be provided to help them make these decisions. Keep in mind that this Governance Committee operates on a different level on a day to day basis than the project level teams that they will be reviewing. If the right level of executives are on the Governance Committee, they will only be familiar with that "50,000 foot view" and corresponding level of detail that goes with it, and they will need support in understanding the basics, such as the expected outcomes of Stage Gates, the criteria for prioritization and why these criteria were selected, and detailed reports that outline the pipeline, potentially broken out into specific types of projects (e.g., early concept, new product development, maintenance), or perhaps a pipeline by specific area within the businesses. However the data is selected to be presented, highlighting the risks as well as the revenue is a necessary element. Pipelines are not always just about the money.

CHAPTER 6

TOOLS & PROCESSES

There are specific tools that assist a well-run Project Management organization do its job even better, yet these tools require more than just Project Management usage and often requires the supporting functions to take an active role in input and management as well.

In the previous chapter, where we discussed Portfolio Management, clearly there is an information system tool that would be critical to hold all this information, but access would need to be severely restricted. The majority of the data used for Portfolio Management comes from the Business Case document, which the Marketing team will quickly learn to manipulate in order to get their projects a higher standing on the prioritization list. Therefore, while the Business Case may be open for updates and changes on a specific schedule, the actual Portfolio Management system should be accessible only to the Portfolio Management team. This ensures data integrity in the PMO organization where objectivity is critical.

Contrary to the Portfolio Management system, a Resource Management system (tool) needs to be open to all the participating functions for their input. There are various resource management tools on the market today to choose from, and the good ones have a minimum of a 20% administrative time buffer built in automatically. This means that only 80% of an individual's time can be allocated to projects. The 20% administrative time includes, vacation, illness, training, meetings, etc., and cannot be considered time available to work on the project. With the tool I utilized during an earlier role, an analysis revealed it was closer to 27% actual administrative time when a pilot group agreed to mark all of their time in the system. With their help, we had a much better grasp on the various administrative activities being captured.

Implementing a resource allocation tool brings a special kind of natural employee suspicion that needs to be overcome. One mistake I made was to look to implement a resource allocation tool in the first months of my new role with the company. There was immediate suspicion that this tool was being implemented as "big brother" and would be used to scout out people who didn't have enough work to do and were skating by.

The communication efforts surrounding the new tool included written and verbal communications, and a continuous underpinning that this new resource tool had absolutely nothing to do with payroll or employee monitoring. The PMO was not looking to see who worked 60 hours or who worked 20 hours that week, it was a matter of understanding the resource needs of the projects versus the available capacity of the individuals who were assigned to work on them. Needless to say, the first few months of data were worthless, until employees realized that we meant what we said and that no one was being called out for not putting in enough, or putting in too many, hours against a project.

What was the proof that turned the tide in our favor and helped employees believe we were not playing big brother and monitoring their output? It was the project prioritization effort which was going on at the same time. Earlier I mentioned that once the projects were in their logical priority order, we drew the budget line to see where the money ran out to fund the projects. When the money ran out, the projects that fell under that line were moved to a buy-up listing to be worked on at a later date, when funding became available. Well, after the budget line was drawn, we also drew a resource line based on the new information we now had from the implementation of the resource tool. This showed where the resources ran out for the projects. This line was even further up the project list than the budget line was, causing multiple other projects to also be moved to the buy-up list for future consideration.

Being able to show where resources ran out, both financial and people, was a true wake-up call to the Governance Team. Now it was no longer that surprising that projects were missing their milestones and running behind schedule. How could they stay on schedule when they didn't have the right number of people (or right skill sets assigned) to get the work done? This realization and resulting change in resource allocation was the main factor behind the improvement in the overall project metrics. With the newly right sized number of projects for the available resources, the work could get done on time and within budget. It really was simple math in the end. What was most surprising was that because there was no resource management or prioritization previously, that there was so little understanding of how many projects were in the pipeline that couldn't possibly be getting any work done, yet everyone believed they were active and ongoing!

The next surprise came when employees began using the tool with genuine time recording of their project efforts. We found individuals allocated at over 200%! And no one was overly surprised that it was usually the best employees that were overallocated. We did tend to see the same names from certain functions on many, many projects – and now we knew why. It seemed the best employees kept being assigned to new projects, while the slower and perhaps weaker employees had less projects to work on.

The functional resource managers, having access to the tool and the reports generated from it, were gently pointed in the direction to see which employees were overallocated and at risk of burn-out. We never pointed out the under allocation – we didn't have to because it was so self-evident in the reports. It was a great outcome to see that some functions were able to give good employees some relief in reallocating work or in hiring new resources as needed.

The resource allocation tool was managed by the Portfolio Management group, but heavily utilized by the Project Managers and the Resource Managers. Project Managers would input the task level information for resources within the projects to assign their time towards and Resource Managers allocated their resources to the projects using the online tool as well. At one point in time, there was well over 3500 individuals using the system.

Twice a year, the Project Management senior leaders held a large group meeting with the functional Resource Managers to review the active projects and the prioritization listing. This all-day meeting gave the

Resource Managers the information they needed to be aware of the any new projects coming and any unusual needs of the existing projects. Always a worthwhile effort, the Resource Managers relied on this meeting to resource and budget their functional needs appropriately, and the Project Managers were able to get the resources they needed without a fight. The additional benefit of having the priority list updated and available for these meetings helped the Resource Managers assign their staff to the most critical projects according to the company objectives without guesswork. In cases where resources were scarce, this was especially helpful to get the right skill sets on the projects that had the highest priority.

Another important process tool in any product driven project environment is the Product Development Process. Believe it or not, not all companies have one. Most regulated companies do, or at minimum have Standard Operating Procedures (SOPs) or Design Control Documents that guide the development process for these medical or pharmaceutical type products. But any product development work can benefit greatly from the availability of a product development guidance document.

This is an area where the true project management purists differ greatly. Most will say that the Product Development Process has to be followed to the letter. My argument is that projects are all different and require different levels of rigor. Excluding regulated products, which absolutely have to follow a prescribed and auditable process, projects that do not require this level of accountability should be given leeway to scale the Product Development Process to the specific needs of that project. This is where the term "guidance" comes in – and if a development process is considered a guidance process, for non-regulated products, then the project gets the flexibility it needs with a governance team that willingly supports the changes the team outlines.

Regardless, all projects benefit from a robust development process that places all associated templates and tools into one place. This one stop shopping for all things product development can be housed on a website, in a SharePoint site or other tool that is supported by the company. We learned that having one person accountable for the maintenance and training of the development process was the most important element of attention we could provide, to keep all the materials up to date and accessible.

While many companies pay dearly to have a Product Development Process implemented by consulting firms, they fall short in maintaining the work after the consultants leave. So much effort goes into the development of the phases/stage gates, project contracts and step descriptions, yet once the implementation is complete, there is seldom much in the way of follow up for maintenance and continuous improvement.

I believe the most valuable part of a solid Product Development Process is the step descriptions. Designed to follow the process outline, each step includes the who, what, where, when and why of each step in the process. Clearly providing links to supporting documentation if needed, a good step description identifies who owns the step, who performs the step, when it should be done and what the inputs and expected outputs are for each item. In an environment where the resources are new or when resources are moved around quickly to support multiple projects, step descriptions can be very valuable.

Key documents of a Product Development Process include a Project Contract, which we discussed earlier as the key governing document for a project, and an Integrated Business Plan (IBP). This Integrated Business Plan is also a dynamic document, much like the Project Contract, which is continuously updated with the status of the functional areas activities. Along with the historical information about the project, the IBP is useful to assess change over time and to track metrics. While the general purpose is to be the one source of truth for the project, where all the data resides in one document, it ultimately functions as a knowledge management tool for new resources to access. Owned by the Project Manager, but contributions are from the assigned functional core team members, the Project Manager keeps the document up to date and available in the designated project repository.

Successful Product Development Process implementations have meaningful and ongoing training associated with them. In fact, a best practice is to have Product Development Process training as part of the onboarding requirements for specific functions since more than likely these new hires will be part of a project team very quickly. This ensures a fast uptake on expectations for learning the process and adherence to requirements of the Product Development Process.

Additionally, I recommend building training decks specific to the needs of the user of the Product Development Process. Starting with an Executive Deck, to be used by you or your Senior Directors to educate the executives on the key elements of the Product Development Process and other PMO processes that they need to be aware of, support or participate in, take the opportunity to meet with these leaders for at least an hour to review the information and gather their feedback. Remember to do this as any executive leadership roles change, since this may happen often, and you should keep these key individuals current on the processes if you want them to remain engaged.

Other decks would include training specifically for the Project Managers, and again specifically for the Core Team Members. I've also seen the training take place just for one functional partner group (e.g., Regulatory Affairs, R&D or Medical), so that there could be an in-depth review of their functions' step descriptions and that expectations could be set for their roles. In some cases, there are activities such as Labeling, where the accountability for this activity lies in multiple areas and is then consolidated into one function. In this instance, or others like it, you would want to call that out for individualized training.

CHAPTER 7

METRICS

Metrics are a key factor in proving your success with your PMO implementation. Yet it is important to start measuring your selected key performance indictors as early as possible, since you can't prove where you've truly made a difference until you know where your starting point was! Take the time to find the baseline of the metrics that you are selecting – this has to be a priority. If the metric you select to measure is currently not measured, then start to measure it immediately, before anyone knows that this will become a key metric for you, since the minute you announce that this is something you will measure, it will instantly get more focus and attention and therefore improve. You want the true baseline, the actual measurement when no one is aware/watching the selected area, before you commit to what the improvement percentage or target can or would be.

First, take the list of the existing metrics available, and don't assume that these are the most important metrics, because likely these are the only metrics that were able to be measured – meaning that the systems currently in place do not allow for more sophisticated tracking. Or it could be that no one ever thought to track project management metrics previously. Either way, your best option is to first know what metrics are available, and then find out which metrics are most important to your key stakeholders.

Before you meet with your key stakeholders about metrics, or if you choose to do this as part of an introductory meeting, be sure you have a list of suggested metrics that you could offer during the discussion.

Most functions are not fully aware of, or interested in, exactly what metrics are important to Project Management. For example, Commercial/Marketing – they could pretty much care less about Project Management metrics – they only want to make sure the product is in their bags and available to sell when it is supposed to be. However, R&D cares about Project Managements metrics very much, and will partner closely with you to get you the data you need to appropriately show accurate status updates. It's pretty amazing though when Senior Management takes a strong interest in metrics how quickly all the various functions get interested and supportive of Project Management metrics.

For large scale projects, I recommend one metric/milestone per quarter. For smaller projects, I suggest one metric/milestone every other quarter. While you do not always have a key metric or milestone to track each quarter for the large-scale projects, you should be able to instead include a leading indicator – a milestone that alerts you in advance if a major deliverable (in a future quarter) is or is not feasible.

In the Early Wins chapter of this book, you will recall that I went into some detail about leading indicators and how this is the measurement of a metric that would indicate if a major metric/milestone/deliverable may or may not be missed based on the achievement of the leading indicator milestone. The example used previously had to do with supplier materials not being ready on time. In the medical device world, a huge leading indicator would be the Regulatory submission date. If that date is missed, then the launch date is more than likely to be missed too! If the FDA doesn't approve the submission on time, you can bet you are not launching the product on the scheduled timeline either.

I want to note that when reporting on milestones, the Launch milestone is clearly the one that everyone remembers. From the point that senior management hears that product launch date for the very first time, it becomes embedded and emblazoned in their memory. Very little else from a deliverables perspective will stick, but no one forgets the first date they hear as the launch date for a product that has a promising revenue involved with it. When tracking all metrics, it was therefore critical that we hold the launch date separately, and track it separately as well. The reason is simply that all projects have problems which can and do push the launch date out. As noted, since no one ever forgets the original launch date, when it does change it is usually due to a major issue or setback – seldom does it change for the better! By keeping the launch dates separate, you keep an accounting of the original launch date and the reasons why it was moved (assuming Project Contract approval was involved), and then everyone can quickly see why that date was changed and know all the reasons behind it. If you fail to do this, you will find yourself peppered with questions in multiple meetings as to why the launch date changed. Keeping track of that level of information mentally, especially when there have been multiple changes and a large portfolio of projects to begin with, is simply not feasible.

Let's talk about the generic types of metrics that can be used. In two basic categories, there are In-Process Metrics (while the product is actually in the development phases) and then the Outcome Metrics, which are the end to end metrics that tell you the performance of the project.

In-Process metrics will provide you with the earliest possible indicators of the trends being experienced in the project. These metrics are used for evaluation and can indicate where process improvements are needed or when the process is working well. Ideally the In-Process metric will give you a heads up that perhaps a deep dive project review is required to investigate the root cause of the issue.

Sample In-Process Metrics include:

- Phase Duration – the time between project phases in a Product Development Process
- Core Team Turnover – the number of changes to the core team members working on a project. The more turnover, the more delays can potentially be experienced due to knowledge transfer and just general competencies of the individuals being swapped out to work on the project
- Milestone Slippage – if a project is continually missing its early milestones, or leading indicator milestones, it's a safe bet that the project may need an intervention to find out what is happening with the team and the product itself. Ultimately you have a clear indicator that the launch date will not be as expected if constant milestone slippage is taking place

- Contract/Charter Stability – depending if your project is utilizing a Project Contract or Project Charter, and assuming that it is being kept up to date by the team and governed by senior management, this is very similar to milestone slippage which would indicate that the project or the team is having major issues. However, while the project may not be missing milestones, it may be having serious risk issues, or a competitive threat may have hit the market unexpectedly or perhaps there are major technology changes taking place. If there is a solid Project Contract in place and governed appropriately, this should trigger a return to governance and a reassessment of the viability of the project

Outcome Metrics, or end to end metrics as they can be called, are measured following the completion of a project. The Core Team members, the various functional organizations and the project governing body at the senior management level, all participate in reviewing these metrics to ensure effective project and product performance.

Sample Outcome Metrics or end to end metrics include:

- New Product Revenue – the expected revenue to be generated by the product once it hits the market and is available for sale. The Project Contract should include this revenue projection and performance should be managed against that projection
- Time to Market – how long it took to get the product from inception into the sales team's bags to sell
- Number of Design Changes Post Launch – the number of design changes within the first year of the product launch
- Throughput of the Pipeline – the ratio of the number of products launched over an X year (normally 5) period versus the total number of projects that were input into the pipeline over that same period of time
- Variances in the project goals related to:
  - Gross Margin
  - Cost Variance in both the product and the project
  - Variance in the forecast/timing

One note about end to end metrics, and this is an absolute pet peeve of mine – is that when a project is completed and the product is launched, there are all kinds of celebrations and rewards and recognition taking place, which is fantastic.   I fully support that there should be rewards and recognition and that the team should be congratulated. What I've seen happen all too often however is that no one looks at the product results 6-12 months down the road to make sure the product is performing as planned and expected.   Seldom is anyone truly looking at the revenue results and measuring that revenue against the original Project Contract expectations. Further, unless there are serious issues with the product, no one is gathering the data regarding complaints until there is a serious problem.

I believe the project team should not be disbanded until one year following the launch of the product. They certainly don't need to meet weekly, but at least monthly for the first 3 months following the product launch and then bi-monthly after that until the one-year post launch mark.   The agenda for these meetings should simply be to review the product progress against revenue expectations and available performance criteria in the market, along with product safety, against the original Project Contract plan.   Having the original team available and monitoring the product makes it so much easier to quickly address issues.   Additionally, the governing body should also be updated on the sales versus the projections at their monthly governance meetings for all projects in the first year of their launch.

As important as collecting the metrics data is, the next step is collecting and reporting this data. This is where the objectivity of a stand-alone PMO comes into play. The ability and willingness to put the data, warts and all, out there for review is what creates the real conversations of what issues may need to be addressed or activities that need to be improved. From there the discussion of how these metrics will be used within the company (to improve the execution of the projects and the ability to make solid decisions regarding both project/product) will follow.

In previous roles, metrics dashboards were provided which showed both the full pipeline metrics roll up of information and then drilled down into metrics by business units, functions and finally by the projects themselves. It would be clear which initiatives/projects were "At

Risk" as a result of the metrics data, and then a further deep dive into these risk areas was undertaken at that point. Normally an "Actions and Status" column was included for each project which included upcoming key milestones and overall commentary from the core team leader on the issues associated with the project. I encouraged core teams to take advantage of this opportunity to put their honest feedback out there to the governing body early and often, to ensure full transparency to any needs of the project.

CHAPTER 8

OUTSOURCING

The trend to outsource work has become very popular in many of the larger companies lately. I say "popular" and did not say "successful". I am aware that a few companies have had good success with outsourcing – and those companies are the ones that have taken the time to carefully understand and plan the work that they will outsource. Successful outsourcing depends heavily on understanding what your core versus non-core work is and releasing the non-core work to be outsourced. And then assigning someone to closely manage the outsourced work.

Core work is where the company is most successful – it is what helps create the company's reputation and why people look to a certain company as a leader in their respective field or with their specific product. Outsourcing any area of core work (e.g., technical knowledge, specific skills), can hurt the company in the long term. However, outsourcing a function such as labeling or documentation control, or a simple manufacturing process, to a company that can do the work for less money, may not hurt a company's reputation and still positively affect the Corporation's financial bottom line through outsourcing to a low-cost service provider.

Successful outsourcing is not only a matter of knowing which work to outsource, but it also requires significant oversight and metrics. A designated individual needs to be assigned to manage the outsource provider, create and follow the agreed upon metrics that prove a successful working relationship and confirm that the outsourced work is being done according to the standards set by the agreement between the two companies. Those companies that outsource work and just assume things are being done as planned, are in for a big surprise when things start to go wrong. Especially those large companies who outsource work that may be required for review during an audit. It's good practice to assign one individual, an Alliance Manager type role, to manage the working relationship, the metrics and the quality and compliance of the work output of the provider. Additionally, during the initial negotiations with the outsource provider, the company should consider supporting both the carrot and the stick approach. Offering the outsource provider incentive (the carrot) to get additional compensation if quality/quantity of work is exceeded and outlining the potential reductions or penalties (the stick) for when it is not.

For Project Management, groups a new trend is emerging – total outsourcing of Project Management. Some Project Management contract houses are being contacted and asked to quote or bid for a full Project Management Organization to support product development teams. Essentially, the contract house would be required to "own" all Project Managers for all of the projects that the Project Managers would be supporting. The Project Managers would be employees of the contract house and not the company they are supporting. The contract house would be responsible for hiring, firing, resourcing, training and movement of the Project Managers.

Do not think of this in terms of general contracting arrangements, where you hire one or more contractors to supplement a project's needs, this is fully outsourcing the Project Management function at the company.

The companies that are requesting this service are looking to jettison not only the headcount costs, but also, in my opinion, the accountability for the success and failure of the projects as well. By viewing Project Management as a service function, the way one would perhaps view the mailroom services, the company takes an entirely myopic view of the skill set involved with Project Management. For example, it's one problem for an outsourced mail services provider to deliver to the wrong mail stop in a company, it quite another issue altogether for a Project Manager to not perform a risk analysis and have a product miss a major milestone. The cost associated with these two examples are worlds apart.

Be that as it may, in an effort to reduce costs, all perceived service functions are at risk for outsourcing regardless of the associated skill set. Human Resources and Training functions are also popular outsourcing targets currently. In the case of Project Managers, it's not just the skill set of Project Management that is lost, it is in many cases years of institutional knowledge that the Project Manager has accumulated from their years of service to the company, in various roles they may have served in during their tenure with the company. When this is lost, or devalued, project results are likely to suffer in the long term. As noted earlier, there are different types of Project Managers – one that supports a Project Leader and one that is a Project Leader. Normally for outsourcing purposes, it would be the Project Manager in the support function that is being looked at for outsourcing. Outsourcing would then include the timeline, charter, contract, risk assessment, meeting management, actions and minutes, etc., Still very difficult to manage – especially if the outsourcing is planned to done remotely, as in a different country altogether.

The quotes for outsourced Project Management that I've seen can be one of many scenarios. Most commonly, the company is requesting that all Project Management employees become employees of the contracting firm and that while they will continue to work on-site for the company they have always worked for (they are still sitting at their same desks in the same company) but now these individuals will be managed by an on-site manager from the outsourced provider and have all salary and benefits converted to the outsourced provider, usually at a bit of a loss to the employee.

New hires to the outsourced provider will come in at a significantly lower salary and with less benefits than those employees that are converted from the previous employer. Benefits will normally stay the same or reduce slightly for the converted employee in the first year of conversion. After that a significant decrease in benefits will start to take place year after year. Of the many major losses to the converted employee will be the size of the annual bonus, any stock options that may have been granted at bonus time as an additional incentive (usually smaller outsourced providers will not have these), and perhaps a hit to the 401k match program as well. The biggest impact however is usually to morale, as the Project Manager no longer sees their role as a value-added contributor to the company, or they wouldn't have outsourced it in the first place.

For the most part, employees who are outsourced and converted to the new provider will stay only as long as it takes for them to find a new position with a different company. And the outsource provider expects that, but wants to be able to retain them for a certain period of time for both continuity and training purposes (training new employees to the outsource provider). The outsourced provider company will not be able to prove initial success if all the newly outsourced employees leave, since the institutional knowledge leaves with them, along with the process knowledge. Very seldom can an outsource provider start from a zero-baseline having no knowledge of the processes or products, teams or culture of the company that it is taking the work from.

The next scenario is offsite outsourcing, where the majority of the current Project Managers are let go and the work is done in another state or possibly even in another country. Those Project Managers who are asked to remain do so with a specific remit to do the training of the new Project Managers, and are usually paid pretty well to do this as the outcome will help ensure the successful transition of work to the new team of Project Managers, wherever they are located. These are usually not long-term assignments for those Project Managers who are asked to stay and train. There is a lure of a retention bonus or additional salary for the initial six months to one year until the projects are underway, and following that, the individuals are either asked to stay on in a management capacity to maintain relationships, or let go after the work is fully transitioned.

In today's global work environment, more and more teams are dispersed and located in various parts of the world. Therefore, the belief is that the project management of the teams can also be done remotely, with the Project Manager supporting and participating by phone or teleconference. Where this usually falls short is culturally, since many teams have a core of individuals who are centrally located and they no longer have a project management anchor, or it can fall short with European countries, who deeply value the face to face element, even if it is only occasional, and being familiar with the team members to help develop the core team comradery.

In a previous chapter, recall the discussion topic of objectivity and how a stand-alone PMO provides that level of objectivity to call out the areas that are not functioning or performing as needed. In an outsource situation this becomes much more finger pointing rather than objective clarity on where a project is failing. The outsource provider does not want to appear as if they are not doing the job necessary to support the team, so the fault has to be positioned with a function or with other members of the team. This leads to many problems in communications, as the core team members will begin bringing up issues to their management rather than within the project team for resolution, which will in turn escalate the issues up to senior management outside of the governance process. Once the team loses faith in their Project Manager, the team becomes dysfunctional and will try to perform as best they can, function specific, to achieve their own project targets rather than the team's project targets.

While outsourcing project management is going to become a rich opportunity for some contract companies as the idea becomes more and more popular, it will be interesting to see the outcomes achieved and the problems associated with outsourcing this key function. I've seen firsthand the results of outsourcing hiring, and the kinds of resumes provided by outsourced HR partners. The time it takes to schedule interviews, test and hire is excessive even assuming you get good candidates to select from. Other unfortunate outsourcing events include training, where the trainer knows less about the topic than the individuals in the room to be trained!

There will be very little you as an individual can do if your company makes the decision to outsource project management. Outsourcing decisions are made at very high levels in the company and it's possible that you will not be in on the decision-making process and it will be a done deal by the time you learn of the plan. These decisions are made on dollars and cents in most cases, and a belief that the company will not suffer any ill effects as a result of the outsourcing, regardless of which functional area is being outsourced. The company leaders will have been shown a cost benefit analysis telling them what their savings will be. If the leadership sees project management as clerical, or has not seen the value add of the project management function as a core attribute that contributes to successful launches, then they are more likely to outsource the role. If you have the opportunity to highlight project management, to deliver project updates to senior managers and to showcase the successful metrics achieved by having project management – it's important to do so early and often to avoid a potential outsource situation if possible. I am confident that once project management is outsourced, it's just a matter of time until it is brought back within the company as most projects will struggle with external and remote project management.

CHAPTER 9

CONTINUOUS IMPROVEMENT

No matter how many different processes you implement when you create a PMO, you can never just rest on your accomplishments, because there is always room to improve. The other consideration is that many times you, as a leader, believe you have implemented strong processes, but in actuality your stakeholders do not feel that way. It's very important to not only make sure that your team and your stakeholders are on board with the new processes/procedures that you are introducing, but just as important that you solicit their ongoing feedback as to the actual effectiveness of your new processes and procedures.

As noted earlier in the book, you should have a few standing meetings set up with your key stakeholders and your own manager, to ensure that you are meeting their expectations. Beyond that however, things change, priorities are updated and what was once important to your functional business partner has been replaced with a new initiative. Staying on top of these changes is important for the PMO leader since you would have no way to know about these changes early enough to be proactive if you wait for the general communication to come out.

Very few items will stay static in a corporate environment. Your team, your tools, all have to be agile enough to quickly adjust to meet the goals of the company when they change or specifically when there is a merger or acquisition announced. Having a plan in place for these activities and being able to motivate your team to engage in these new actions without losing steam on what they are currently working on is sometimes difficult to manage.

Being able to implement continuous improvement within the PMO confirms your willingness to support the overall organization. To be effective, both you and your team should be well versed and trained in Change Management principles, or in rare cases, have the ability to bring in a Change Management expert (consultant) to get your team through the first few months of these significant changes with a solid plan in place.

An example of continuous improvement would be the introduction of a new role within the PMO. Seeing a need for better execution during product launches, a new role was created called a Launch Project Manager. The responsibility of this role was after the product development was completed, but onboarding the new Project Manager just prior to the launch of the product. This entailed the hand-off of project management responsibilities during the Validation phase of the project. The development Project Manager would begin working with the Launch Project Manager during this late project phase, and then hand off the project to the Launch Project Manager after the first site received product and was considered "launched". The Launch Project Manager would take the team through the first year of the product launch, ensuring the launch process was carefully adhered to in the various regions that the product was scheduled to be launched. Additionally, they would manage the deliverables of the original Project Contract and the promised metrics in sales and performance.

This role was a true departure from the development Project Manager who currently focused solely on the project during the actual development phases. Too often the team disbanded after the first launch and there was no management of the metrics that were expected. The Launch Project Manager had accountability for the successful regional launches as well as oversight of the metrics and complaints. Keeping someone fully focused on the first-year launch activities also confirmed that the team would be kept together, albeit on a less regular meeting schedule, but maintaining a connection to the project and staying invested in the outcomes. This Launch Project Manager role is specifically valuable when the company's pipeline is heavily back-end loaded, with multiple launches expected during a fiscal year.

Another continuous improvement activity that was implemented around year 4 after the introduction of the PMO, was a full refresh of training with our cross-functional partners, core teams and stakeholders, to address process erosion. Process erosion naturally takes place over time due to various reasons: attrition being a main reason, since people move on, change roles and perhaps retire or leave the company for better opportunities. Perhaps the bigger reason was because people had learned how to circumvent the processes over a period of 4 years. Let's face it – some people do not like process and have to find a way around it. Refreshing the training, making the effort with the stakeholders and within the teams to re-train and re-focus on process was necessary to get the processes back into alignment, while training new individuals on how to be successful using the tools we had already introduced. This was not a small effort. There was a great deal of planning, renewing training decks/presentations and meeting scheduling that had to be done. By far the most successful training took place during staff meetings, and we asked for time at our functional partner's upcoming staff meetings to specifically refresh skills and inform on process changes. The additional benefit to this was hearing our partner's concerns and why they felt certain aspects of the processes were either not working, or taking too long to get them what they needed. Essentially, we learned "why" the circumventing of the processes was taking place, and we were able to remediate those issues along the way.

An area that was ready for continuous improvement was the Sustaining work. Sustaining work is any work that is being done on product that is already available on the market. There is nothing remotely exciting about Sustaining work, and this is clear to everyone who works on these products. For the most part, the work is addressing corrective or preventative actions, supplier changes, line extensions or perhaps a change to some functionality with the product. No one fights to be on a Sustaining project team, except at one very large company I worked for – where to be accepted onto a Sustaining project team was considered an honor. You could only work on a Sustaining project if you were the "best of the best". Why? Because the on-market products are what pays your paycheck and keeps the company afloat. These products are the reputation of the company and why people buy the brand. Yes, this massive company had it right, and had great people working on Sustaining activities and rewarded them very well. If more companies had that mindset, you wouldn't have individuals dissatisfied with working on these on-market products and could generate much more excitement and enthusiasm around this work.

With the introduction of prioritization for the new product development work, it would naturally follow that we would move to prioritize the Sustaining work as well. And we did. This required a massive overhaul in the structure of the Sustaining teams and how the work was accepted into the Sustaining project pipeline. We quickly recognized that much of the work was being done on very low selling or low volume products, which led to decisions on whether or not to even keep the product alive and active, or that work was being done region specific, meaning that it had little impact on sales as well, except for in one or two specific regions. The priority was clearly to always work on safety related or compliance issues first, and headcount and funds were directed accordingly. All of this was done through an internally developed online tool which everyone had access to. The tool would divert the project request to the appropriate Sustaining team and the team would prioritize according to the information provided. The highlight of this continuous improvement was the visibility gained into the work that was being done on low value products, which launched a separate initiative in Marketing to begin to address the need to discontinue some products completely and focus funds and resources against better selling and better performing products.

Finally, for the PMO team members, we updated the PMO competency assessment model. The first PMO competency assessment was done in year one of the PMO implementation. Since the first attempt was met with suspicion as to the intent and outcome of the assessment, this continuous improvement update to the competency assessment was instead met with anticipation and support. Since the leadership team acted on the results of the first assessment, creating training plans and individual development plans, this time employees knew that their input would be valued and acted upon too. The results were much better as far as an improvement in the individuals perceived skills and competencies, and far more aligned in the gap that was presented between the employee's assessment and their manager's assessment of their skills. More importantly, utilizing continuous improvement as the reason to re-do the competency assessment for the Project Managers was received as a positive reinforcement that their leaders remained invested in their skills and ongoing development needs.

Continuous improvement can be applied to every aspect of the organization; people, process and products. The ability to keep a focus on continuous improvement is the challenge. With the many day-to-day activities that every leader is faced with, it takes a dedicated effort and self-reminder to sit down with your leaders and hold this exercise to identify which areas of continuous improvement need to be addressed, and then making it part of your goals to do so.

CHAPTER 10

MENTORING

There are two roles within the Mentoring function; Mentor and Mentee. While most of my experience has been in the Mentor capacity, I do want to take you back to the Jurassic period of my career and tell you about a few individuals who had the greatest impact on my career and my leadership style.

Coming from a very sports minded family on both sides, with my father being a minor league baseball player during the late 1940's, my sister and I both excelled at basketball. While in high school, besides playing basketball and attending basketball camps as often as I could, in school I took all the optional business classes, including typing, stenography (which no one even knows about anymore) and keypunching. Few people recognize that term anymore either, but it was early data input, punched on long index like cards, then fed into an enormous computer. My teacher, a wonderful southern lady named Mrs. Elizabeth Marsh, trained me on the keypunch machine that was located in a small backroom behind the main classroom. It just so happened that this is how the report card information was input and then run at the computer at the local community college.

When word of that extra-curricular assignment leaked, you can easily imagine the number of monetary offers (and date requests) that I received from the jocks looking to pass their courses, but I never gave in. The point is that Mrs. Marsh was the first one to realize that I had a head for business and she wanted to give me a leg up with learning this new (now ancient) keypunch machine and keypunching process which included programming a card with special punches that would tell the computer what input to expect, which eventually let me walk right into my first job at a local company in their keypunch department. Of interest, at that time we were paid by our keystrokes per hour, with 10,000 keystrokes per hour being the goal.

Shortly thereafter, I joined Western Electric, and was assigned to Bell Laboratories. A fantastic opportunity and back then, and assumed to be a lifetime job. Western Electric became AT&T, which spun off Lucent, which spun off Agere, became LSI, and I honestly don't know any more what remains of Bell Labs, but it was a wonderful place to work, outstanding people and management, paid for my college education and gave me 22 years of experience that shaped my career. I could write a book about those 22 years alone, and the amazing technologies, cleanrooms, company history and risqué 3rd shift stories. That time truly was the highlight of my entire working career.

Starting as a clerk, then moving into an executive assistant role (I still did not have my undergraduate degree yet), I worked for a Marketing VP who was as smart as he was demanding. I was much quieter back then, I simply just dug in and got the work done, and always went the extra mile and added my own spin to the work I was doing if I felt it was adding value. One day my boss mentioned that I should now attend his staff meetings and that I would be responsible for gathering and then regularly reporting certain information and metrics. I remember looking at him and blurting out "I can't do that", because to me, I didn't want to speak up nor present, in front of a group of people. He simply looked up and said, "you'll do it, or you're fired", and put his head right back down into his work. I remember just walking out of his office stunned, then I got angry, and then I did the presentation just to prove to him that I could. He worked closely with me to ensure that I didn't fail and continued to provide new learning opportunities for me to develop my managerial skills. Years later he finally told me that he gave me that initial pushy directive just to make me mad, because he wanted to shake me out of my comfort zone and move me into a better position, and he eventually did, which then launched my management career.

And finally, once I continued to go through the management ranks, and finished my degree, I was fortunate enough to transfer to a new role and work for an exceptional female Vice President who mentored me and specifically helped me to shape and then refine my style in leadership, interacting and negotiating with senior leaders and managing subordinates. She was direct, forthright, and had a laugh that would shake the room – you just didn't expect that this kind of roaring laugh would come out of this woman by the way she looked, so incredibly polished and professional. One day I realized that so few people had heard her let loose with that laugh, and then I realized that you had to be good friends with her to get to experience it. She was patient and shared her career experiences with me. She shot straight from the hip and pulled no punches with her colleagues, with her staff and with her boss. She was unapologetic for what she expected, she worked for it and she was not going to ask twice for what she knew she deserved. I will always value her friendship and I still feel her influence often and I am grateful that she had that strong of an effect on me. Sadly, she passed away at a young age due to complications from a freak accident, and I never had the chance to thank her for the guidance she gave to me. If I close my eyes and concentrate, I can still hear that wonderful laugh!

As my career progressed and I began to mentor individuals, I learned that it was important to set the expectations early and upfront for how the mentoring relationship would work. This as a result of one of my very first mentees sitting down with me for the first time and saying to me, "so, what are you going to do for me"? I had to tell her that this wasn't how it worked at all – that mentoring was a supporting relationship and that I would help talk through her goals, her development plan, her challenges and her opportunities, while providing my experience and support for her to consider. If I could open a door for her along the way, I'd be happy to do that, but ultimately her career was her responsibility, and that mentoring was not me being assigned to get her the next promotion. Fortunately, she decided she needed a different mentor. Fortunately for me.

Mentoring can be either formal or informal as well. I worked for companies that had formal mentoring networks, where actual mentor/mentee assignments were introduced for a defined time period. This usually worked quite well, since if the company was large enough, you were able to work with and mentor individuals who were not in your direct line of reporting yet they may have an interest in the functional area that you were leading. It was also good to get a different perspective on the education and the goals of the mentees from the various organizations and for the mentee to get a better understanding of some of the functions that they were not normally exposed to as part of the role they currently held.

Less known however was the informal women's network that was taking place within the formal mentoring network itself. Now, I am not a feminist by any stretch. If I was, I would have been retired very young and very rich from an incident early in my career, well before sexual harassment or workplace discrimination ever became a common term. I do however believe that women who do the same work as a man does should be paid the same, promoted with the same speed and given the same level of respect as any man in a commensurate role. It shouldn't matter if you are female, male, what color you are, where you went to school, who you marry or who you pray to – fair is fair. Yet back then, it wasn't always the case.

This informal network, and a tactic I still use today when mentoring a really strong candidate, was for the female leaders to arrange for a meeting with their mentee and other female leaders (in other functions which may be of specific interest to the mentee) to explore potential openings. Not current openings, but future, potential positions. This serves two purposes; first, the introduction is made, the mentee has an opportunity to ask what kind of skills or specialized training may be needed for the role and whether or not this is or is not a role that they would like to pursue in the future if indeed a position opened up in this function. Secondly, with no real opening on the table during the discussion, it truly becomes a conversation about what that leader's function contributes to the overall company. It's a genuine information sharing session where the leader gets to talk about their organization and the mentee gets the amazing chance to put themselves in front of this leader to be considered for future opportunities. If this conversation goes well, you can bet that the leader is going to call this individual when the next opening appears. It's a win/win situation, but it has to be well planned out.

I provided my mentees a list of ten questions to go into the meeting with, in case the conversation wanes or does not go as planned. Normally only three or four of the questions ever get used, because this is not an interview, there is no opening to discuss – it's about what the organization does and the mentee exploring if this is a function they would like to pursue in the future.   The ten questions can certainly be used in an interview situation too, and I include them below for reference.

1. What does your department/organization contribute to the overall bottom line of the company?
2. What do you feel the strongest value of your department/organization to the business unit you support (or if global, to the overall company)?
3. What are you most proud of about your department/organization?
4. What is the level of education, or the type of skills you expect, for individuals to bid into your department/organization?
5. How long do individuals typically remain in your group?
6. What are the biggest changes that have occurred in your department/organization over the past few years (or since this manager has taken over the group)?
7. How does your department/organization typically react to change?
8. What can you tell me about your leadership style and what you look for in people who would like to join your department/organization?
9. How long does it usually take for someone to ramp up in your department/organization to the point where they are fully onboarded and working on their own?
10. How do you assess success in your staff members?   What is it that differentiates your highest performing team members in your opinion?

I guided my mentees to end their discussion with not only their thanks for the leader taking the time to meet with them, but with a clear yes or no as to whether or not this is a functional area that they would or would not like to pursue in the future.   The mentees find this tough to say, so I will instead ask the question myself to the mentee by saying "so, is this an area you can see yourself wanting to work in the future if something should come up"? But mentees should be able to say that for themselves, and to have that confidence and courage to tell a leader that they would want to work for them at some point, or not.

This informal network was responsible for a good amount of movement of mentees into new roles. While initially this was done with the female leaders, over time it expanded to include all managers, since it was found to be a valuable introductory tool for mentees to meet other leaders and find out more about their organizations. After all, what leader doesn't love to talk about what their organization does and how it contributes to the company? We all do – and when there is no job on the table, no actual interview taking place, to be able just to meet and talk with someone who may have interest in the group is a welcome opportunity for both the leader and the mentee.

The other informal method I've seen utilized is where an individual approaches you specifically, outside of any formal or designated mentoring program, and simply asks if you will mentor them. While I have often said yes to this request, there have been a few times when I've said no to this request. Recently when I just had too many mentees to give enough attention to all the needs of the individuals and previously, when it felt to me like an opportunistic request, or when I had previous knowledge of the individual asking multiple leaders for mentoring support, perhaps an entitlement issue where they feel they should be in a better role, or are unhappy with their manager and want to pull that relationship issue into the mentoring process. Sometimes you just have to say no.

Also, don't discount that you as the mentor are the only one teaching in this mentoring relationship. As much as people complain about the Millennials, and I've raised two myself so I better not be one of the complainers, I was happily surprised when I happened to mention a technical problem I was having with finding a software I needed during a mentoring session that not only did my Millennial mentee know exactly what I was looking for, he installed the software and taught me how to use it.

If you are looking to approach an individual to be your mentor, don't do this until you are certain of that individual's credibility and standing within the company. You've heard the terminology about "hitching your wagon" or "riding their coattails", and you will want to be sure you don't become tainted with guilt by association if there is a situation where the mentor you are selecting is not being held in particularly high esteem at the moment. You're looking for support, thoughtful guidance and a sounding board from a respected leader and hopefully this leader is one who wants to mentor as well. Women tend to be toughest on other women, and I will honestly say that I became a better mentor when I knew I had hit my glass ceiling. At that point, it became easier for me to mentor objectively and from the heart since I no longer had a stake in improving my own position in the company.

If you approach an individual to mentor you and they decline, don't be discouraged and don't take it personally. Some leaders are just not cut out to be mentors or simply do not have the time or inclination to do it. Therefore, they would not mentor well anyway and you are better off finding someone who has your best interests in mind and the time to spend with you. It's their loss to not have the opportunity to mentor.

The final thought on mentoring is to not waste time if the mentor/ mentee relationship isn't working or is strained. Even after a discussion about expectations, if either person feels the mentoring relationship is a chore, or a requirement, then it's time to call it off – no harm, no foul. It shouldn't be taken personally, sometimes people just don't hit it off and one or the other is not getting what they need, or do not have the time to contribute to the mentor/mentee relationship. Even in a good mentor/mentee relationship, put a finite end date in place right away when initially discussing the expectations for the relationship. The mentoring relationship should not exceed one year. It seems to automatically become strained after that point. That's not to say you can't catch up and meet for lunch every so often, but the formal relationship needs to have a completion date to give both the mentor and the mentee the ability to move on and work with others as well to expand their experiences.

CHAPTER 11

THE EVOLUTION OF THE PROJECT MANAGER ROLE

I have been fortunate enough to truly see the evolution of the Project Manager role firsthand. Following a year-long assignment on 3rd shift supervising an integrated circuit cleanroom, I was asked to change roles and move into the Information Technology (IT) department.

The reason I was asked to move into the IT department was because there were plans for a very large-scale company spin-off on the horizon. I was working for AT&T at the time and the spin-off was Lucent Technologies. For readers old enough to remember this event, this was a highly anticipated and lucrative spin-off, encompassing Bell Laboratories and other divisions into an entirely new company. Lucent Technologies no longer exists today, having had spin-offs of its own and ultimately being acquired by other companies over the years, but back then, it was an exciting opportunity to be asked to become a member of the spin-off team.

Being closely familiar with the inner workings of Manufacturing and the cleanroom environment, the request for me to move to IT was to support the spin-off by leading one of the MES (Manufacturing Execution Systems) teams. All team leaders were asked to take the Project Management courses that AT&T was going to bring in-house for us through the Steven's Institute of Technology.

There were either eleven or twelve courses all together, each averaging about one week in duration and it was expected that we were to take at least one to two of the courses a month either in-house at our local AT&T work location facility or drive to the New Jersey training center. Upon completion, we received a Master's Certification in Project Management from Steven's Institute of Technology and were considered eligible and prepared to take the PMI (Project Management Institute) PMP (Project Management Professional) exam. Preparing for and taking the actual PMP exam was at each individual's discretion and was not required by AT&T at the completion of the training courses. I believe the goal of AT&T in taking on the massive expense of training so many individuals in Project Management was to deliver the fundamentals of the Project Management concepts and ensure that we all had the foundational knowledge necessary to interact well with our teams and with each other during the spin-off activities.

The training provided was very specific to the PMBOK (Project Management Book of Knowledge) guidelines, and taught each step of the process and the various knowledge areas. Since the trainees were all from AT&T, our program included exercises and examples that were specific and relevant to our products and processes, which was incredibly helpful in understanding the various intricate details of creating critical paths and work breakdown structures.

Where AT&T was ahead of its time with the Project Management role was that they expected the Project Manager to lead the team, not just support the team by developing project plans and risk assessments. The selection of the team leaders being individuals intimately familiar with the working areas that they were going to be involved in spinning off was incredibly forward looking and likely responsible for the success of the systems separation.

I should note that the IT system separation (from AT&T to Lucent) all took place on one day; this was called a "flash cut", and at the time, the largest flash cut ever attempted for such a large company. There were multiple rehearsals, called "a day in the life" testing where the cutover activities were rehearsed around the globe, and individuals tested the new system for a full day and tried to find any bugs or flaws in the system that may need to be repaired. These IT systems included all financial, human resource and manufacturing systems, and the scale of the testing and training involved was enormous. The fact that it was a completely successful flash cut of all IT systems is a testament to the training received and the preparation involved by all participants.

Project Management had long been viewed as a supporting role, the individual who would develop the project plan and schedule team meetings and issue meeting minutes. For those Project Managers who were happy in that supporting capacity, the evolution into the Project Manager as Team Leader role did not sit well with them and they struggled to develop the skill set necessary to lead and manage a project team.

I mentioned earlier that many individuals became Project Managers by osmosis. These individuals were never actually trained in Project Management. There was a need for a Project Manager and perhaps their role was being eliminated and they were an organized person and it was felt that they could do a good job in this new role and therefore they were placed into the role. Some individuals embraced the role and learned all that they could, and others simply saw the role as a job to keep a paycheck coming. I know many successful Project Managers who never chose the role for themselves yet ended up making a successful career out of it.

The expectation of leading the project was not in the initial Project Manager position description. Not everyone wants to lead, that's a personal preference and that desire needs to be respected. You cannot force someone to lead others; there is no opportunity for success in that scenario. For those individuals who prefer the supporting side of Project Management versus the leadership angle, there are roles that can and should be created to accommodate that skill. In previous companies, these roles were called Project Coordinators.

The change to Project Managers as Team Leaders came about as a result and outcome of many downsizing activities that were taking place. As companies looked to improve their financial bottom line, as more mechanized and robotic systems were installed, Project Mangers evolved to become technical experts as well as Team Leaders. In taking on these additional responsibilities, the value of the role increased exponentially. It wasn't just Project Managers who had to adjust and take on new responsibilities. I can recall the term "slashers" being given to Engineers who would now take on the supervision of certain staff as well as their existing engineering responsibilities. Hence the term "slasher", meaning Engineer/Supervisor. For the Project Manager, it became Project Manager/Team Leader.

The initial conflicts of the Project Manager as team leader function came in multiple forms. If the project had a Project Sponsor, depending on the level of involvement the Project Sponsor had with the project, they felt a bit put off by the new Project Leader. Until the role of Project Sponsor was fully defined, and not an abstract concept of both Leader and Sponsor, there was a bit of tension between the two roles. Today, that tension doesn't exist. The role of Project Sponsor, in the rare cases where a Project Sponsor is active (usually very large scale or high priority projects), is normally a high-level executive, who can remove barriers and stays abreast of the project status through informational updates. While this can be incredibly useful and valuable for key projects, a Project Sponsor is certainly not required for the mid to low level projects that can basically run with general project governance.

As a general rule, in larger companies where there are multiple divisions or project focus areas, Project Managers tended to stay within one division. While this was valuable to the Project Manager in becoming an expert in a specific product area, it could also stagnate the Project Manager and limit their ability to move between divisions to expand their growth potential and ultimately their job security.

As a PMO Leader, I wanted to take the opportunity to move Project Managers across multiple divisions to provide those growth opportunities. However, there were individuals who wanted to stay within their current focus areas and comfort zones. This is a personal preference which I can fully understand, and depending where you are in your career progression (for example, late in your career) then perhaps it is right where you need to be. Always be aware that the trade-off could come suddenly, when a division is disbanded because a product area is no longer viable, or perhaps a division is spun off or sold off. At that point in time you will only be able to rely on your actual Project Management skills to move into a different group, since your technical knowledge of the now no longer viable product area will have little value. Opportunities for career growth and movement can be discussed and presented to the employee, but ultimately every individual makes their own choices.

Evolution in Project Management was also largely a result of the speed which technology enabled over the past 20 years. The Project Manager had to learn new systems and tools and be able to communicate and present the outcomes to upper management. The tools (i.e., MS Project, SharePoint, Risk Applications, etc.) provided much needed visibility to the project needs and status, but few companies allotted the necessary time to the learning curve which was required to master these new tools and systems.

Thrust into leading a team, utilizing every new application that some senior leader decides that this is how they want material presented to them, while working in what is now a much more global environment (team members all over the world), Project Managers quickly learned that flexibility was going to be key in how projects were managed going forward.

In the past, Project Managers followed the PMBOK religiously and each step description in the Product Development Process regardless of value or requirement. Now, faced with continuous status report updates and rapidly changing technologies, the project timelines were changing constantly and it was becoming difficult to keep up all deliverables.

Smart Project Managers adapted quickly, and learned to leverage all project materials and existing project repositories to keep their senior leaders informed and aware of the progress of the project, while evaluating the needs of the project and scaling the project plan to the absolute necessities required to complete the project successfully. The added focus on metrics management only contributed further to the stress on the Project Manager, since every deliverable and result was now being measured and tracked.

If I could go back in time and ask a manager in the 1980's what a Project Manager role includes, I'm sure they would talk about task level management and creating project plans and checking the boxes of what needs to be done on a project off a list. There would be discussion about creating meeting agendas, meeting minutes and following up on action items. Ask today's manager what a Project Manager does and you should get quite a different outcome assuming you are working in a progressive company.

Today's Project Manager leads, assesses, communicates and creates the environment for project success utilizing technology and their own knowledge base about the product/project. Project Managers are strategic and savvy executors of the project requirements, coordinating team efforts to complete the project on time, within scope and quality, and on budget. Those project tenants have not changed (time, scope, quality, cost), but the Project Manager has evolved into owning those tenants, and having the accountability for the overall success of the team and the project outcomes.

CHAPTER 12

NETWORKING & SELF-DEVELOPMENT

In the last chapter, I talked about Project Managers who preferred to stay within their comfort zones of a specific product or knowledge area. Possibly these are Project Managers who are late in their careers and they do not need nor want any further exposure to new opportunities. In this chapter, we will discuss where early career professionals need to remain open to opportunities in various areas and how this will expand their network and increase their visibility within the company.

I'm writing from the perspective of relatively large companies, therefore the assumption in my writing is that there are multiple opportunities and areas for growth where you are working. In the event that you are working in a small company with limited mobility, that's fine too! This is about understanding your opportunities where you are today and if you need to scale that to a different level or if this helps you to recognize that the growth you seek is not available where you are working today, these are all choices that you need to think through. Ultimately you are the only one who knows where you are happiest and most fulfilled with your day to day work. Where you work, what you do and what matters most to you is your decision alone and one that you have to be comfortable with 20 years from now.

In the working environments that I have experienced in my career, there have been exceptional opportunities for growth. From AT&T's rotational program, where you worked for a maximum of 3 years in a certain function or role, to previous companies that had Talent Steering Committees (TSC) at the highest levels of the organization to help develop high potential employees, I've seen employees who have put themselves out there to be noticed and I've seen others, strong performers, who wait for someone in senior leadership to notice them.

When I was introduced into AT&T's rotational program, I was told that if I were to stay in one function/role for more than 5 years, the odds of my being successful in a different department or role within AT&T would be very slim, simply because other employees would not be able to see me in a different capacity. Think about that, someone you know who has been working at one position for so long that you couldn't possibly see them doing anything else other than that specific role. I bet you can think of quite a few people in that scenario!

That was great advice for me early on in my career, since I did not, at that time, have any confidence in my abilities nor did I know which function would really suit me and satisfy my career aspirations. Having the ability and expectation to rotate into various functions was the permission I needed to not feel as if I was letting anyone down by leaving a certain role or department. In leading a new PMO, I openly discussed with new or transferring employees to the PMO that I wanted them to give me 2 years in the role, and if they decided to stay in Project and Portfolio Management, I'd be thrilled to keep them. But, after 2 years, if they decided that Project Management wasn't for them and they wanted to try something else, I would do everything I could to help them move into a new role in the area they wanted to try next. This really surprised a lot of employees, since most leaders felt personally insulted when individuals left their organization, therefore the employees felt obligated to stay.

In the Project Manager role, the exposure that you receive to the various functions that you work with on the project team inherently introduces you to those areas and to the type of work that they are responsible for. Let's take an example of the Regulatory Affairs function. During the day to day project activities and development of the project plan, you learn what tasks and activities the Regulatory Affairs team member is accountable to perform and how long it takes to create a product submission to the FDA for a medical device or how the Regulatory Affairs group needs to react when a regulation changes. If this intrigues you, and you believe this is an area you would like to explore future career opportunities, why would any good leader hinder your growth?

Holding this open discussion early in the introduction stage to the PMO gave employees that same permission to stay open to exploring other functions and opportunities while also letting them know that I hoped they would chose to stay with the PMO.

The early career professionals today don't require that same level of permission, they already know that they can and should be open to new opportunities. They are well aware that companies and roles can change rapidly and that no future opportunities or job security is promised. There is a bit of a role reversal today from my early career when I wanted to know what I could do for the company to move myself ahead. Today the question is about what the company can do for them (the early career professional) and what will the company do to keep them happy?

The larger companies have responded well to this new way of keeping early career professionals engaged. Early talent/career networks or resource groups are now very active and have their own senior level sponsorship and events in many companies. Events are focused toward networking and often include speakers that talk about Work/Life Balance or panels of senior leaders that openly discuss their career progression. I've personally participated in events where I was asked to detail out my organization, the roles and how the organization contributes to the company bottom line. I've outlined the PMO processes and the expected skill sets of the roles in the organization. These informational events are focused towards continually engaging the early career professional and providing ongoing opportunities to network and to learn.

If your company has resource groups, and these can vary by interests or focus areas, I highly recommend participating and opening yourself up to the opportunities that these resource groups can present. Within smaller companies that do not have these resource groups, then there is always the potential to look outside to join external groups that have a focus area that interests you specifically. For Project Managers, there is a wealth of external community groups to consider, along with webinar participation and large event offerings.

Participating in or potentially joining sub-teams within the existing company resource groups are excellent resume builders and show employers your willingness to step up and speak up on behalf of your special interest areas. Often these resource groups provide leadership and speaking opportunities for you to help develop your skills and improve your comfort level in discussions with large groups. These networking opportunities are the kind of quick self-development opportunities that you can take advantage of easily.

Networking isn't just about job hunting, although don't discount the value of a strong network when the job hunting need arises. Your network is your ally for questions about other companies, best practices, functional expertise, just to name a few. Don't just connect with individuals you know or have worked with previously on LinkedIn, keep engaged and involved with them if you can on a regular basis. This will be beneficial when it comes time to ask for help with the tough questions or with job hunting. Keep your professional network professional on all levels. Don't confuse your professional network with your friends, the two should be very separate.

Networking is also about staying open to new ideas and new technologies. You can read and learn about new systems and tools, but knowing someone on the inside, who can walk you through the usage or the background, is invaluable. Placing yourself into a position of learning, regardless of what stage of your career you are in, through attendance at various meetings and events, gives you an opportunity to open up your network outside of the work environment.

Inside of the work environment, one of the best networking tools that I've taken advantage of is break time or lunch time. How often do you take your lunch back to your desk and eat alone while you catch up on emails? What value is that providing to your networking capabilities?

As a Project Manager, I took advantage of inviting team members individually to coffee or to have lunch together to discuss the project. Ideally, I wanted to get each team members perspective about the project, the progress of the project, the health of the team, where improvements could be made, etc. This one on one discussion allowed for the opportunity to learn about what their project level concerns were while also creating a much-needed personal relationship with the individual. I wanted the team member to know that I was there to hear their concerns and react to them if it was something I could affect. I wanted to open the door to further discussions and to have that comfort level between us so that issues could be openly discussed.

In a team environment, not everyone is comfortable speaking up, especially if they believe it will result in a conflict. That's why these one on one discussions were so valuable. I could hear first-hand what the issues were, and develop the relationship with that individual in the process. This effort benefitted both the project and my network, and was simple and easy to implement. Giving individuals a completely non-threatening environment to share their thoughts and concerns is an opportunity for you to build trust and build relationships. Take advantage of the chance to get to know your team members, you're going to be surprised at what you will learn and how much more effective you can be when you hear their ideas and perspectives.

Self-development is a natural progression coming from understanding where you want to go with your career. Gaining the personal insight of knowing what roles you would like to pursue in the future helps you to define what types of skills you need to develop and what additional knowledge you need to acquire to get to where you want to be in the future.

The Project Manager gets the unique perspective of seeing other functional team members roles and what they do. They develop an understanding of what that team member must know, what skills they must have, to perform the project activities to succeed. Yet the Project Manager needs to be very careful not to assume that this is the only work that these functional team members do. More often than not, being on a project team is just one element of the team members role, and there are many tasks and activities that the Project Manager never sees. That's why it is very critical to understand your team members tasks and their capacity constraints. If you believe that the only work they do is on the project team, then why isn't the project work getting done on time? It's because there are so many other expectations on your team members along with their assigned project work.

If you are not in the Project Manager role, then learning about these other functional areas becomes a more difficult task, and this is where either your network or possible mentoring options should come into play for you. It will be important for you to dig deep into understanding what your target role includes, and what skill sets are required to do it. To find this information out, you will need to reach out to someone working in the role today and have a good discussion. Through mentorship, you may be able to get connected with someone from your target organization or possibly request to "shadow" the individual for a few days. Shadowing is spending a few days or a week or more with the individual while they do their day to day work. You would attend meetings with them, spend time in their office space or cubicle and see what activities they perform on a regular day at work.

However you chose to learn more about the target role/area that interests you, keep focused on the skills and knowledge required to do the role and how you can go about gaining that particular information. I am a strong proponent of rotational assignments and would suggest that you ask for a short rotation in an area of interest. Occasionally, some functions can get overwhelmed because of a specific initiative or project. You can go to your manager and offer that you could assist that function with your support for a short period of time, giving you the opportunity to learn about the work up close. This opportunity can confirm that this is a role you will enjoy and will not be disappointed with and stuck there for a period of time should you take a position in that function. I've been there; two horrible years in a department that I detested walking into every day with work that I didn't enjoy. I was locked in for 2 years and I made it through, but I learned my lesson and heavily researched new opportunities before I moved into future roles. Everyone makes mistakes with their career; forgive yourself and move on as soon as you can. It's still an experience to list on the resume.

If your ultimate goal is to land a role in senior leadership, bear in mind that you will need diverse and varied experiences in multiple roles on your resume. Seldom do senior leaders come from and stay in one specific functional area for their entire career. For most senior leaders, they have experience in both technical and support functions, with a helpful understanding or time spent in the Finance realm. That time you spent in that awful role in Purchasing that you couldn't wait to get out of? This becomes solid experience and understanding of an area that will help you land that senior leadership position in the future.

Years ago, I did not have at my fingertips the information available today on the internet. With a few keystrokes, you can be connected to resources and information about any area that interests you. Today, I use the resources available on the internet to research topics for insights and alternative methodologies for processes. Self-development is just that; having the ambition and desire to learn more about a specific topic or activity to improve your knowledge and expertise. It takes discipline, but if you want something badly enough you will focus on finding those resources that will assist you in getting what you want. Don't wait for opportunities to come to you, go find them and learn the skills you need to succeed in these roles. The information available on the internet today has never been better.

In larger companies, development opportunities can be managed through the Human Resources function and within the senior leadership teams for specific functional areas. As an example, the Chief Financial Officer (CFO) and his direct reports would meet on a monthly basis to review the following agenda topics as part of their Talent Steering Committee meetings:

- Slating opportunities for Director level and higher openings within the CFO function (placement of high potential individuals into key roles)
- Metrics related to regrettable loss and general loss due to attrition. (regrettable loss differs from natural attrition in that you identify individuals who have left your organization that you really didn't want to lose in any position or capacity or a previously identified high potential employee)

- Inclusion & Diversity Metrics for the organization (usually pre-identified metrics provided by the Human Resources organization)
- Open Positions Review (discussion and approval for open head-count requests within the organization)
- Leadership Training Plans (alignment of corporate training plans or discussions regarding specific training to be provided to the organization).
- High Potential employee reviews (activities related to the identified high potential employees which can include defined mentoring opportunities, targeted one on one conversations, specific presentations on individuals and their skills and/or adding visibility opportunities for high potential employees)
- Additional considerations this team could review would be the ability to implement a Competency Assessment within the high potential group of individuals or possibly an overall implementation within the entire organization)

Once you are identified as a high potential employee in a large company, there are many opportunities that may open up for you. The expectations on you will be high for your ongoing personal performance to remain in the high potential group. How do you know that you have been identified as a high potential employee within your company? Chances are you will not be told implicitly that you are on "the list". However, if you achieve and maintain the highest performance level, notice that you receive special attention with mentoring possibilities and/or are offered high visibility assignments, potential rotational opportunities, etc., then it's a fair bet to say you have likely been identified as a high potential candidate.

If you are not in the above categories and want to know how to get there; go directly to your manager and find out what you need to do to stand out and get noticed. Managers should not be shy about telling you where you need to improve, what additional skills you may need to acquire or what other experiences would assist in helping you achieve high potential status within the company. If your manager is waiting until your year-end review to tell you how you are doing, that's too late.

Your performance review discussions should be taking place at least on a bi-monthly basis. If this is not happening, make it happen during your one on one or status update meetings with your manager. This is within your control and you should absolutely be on top of your performance status on a regular basis.

While an identified high performing employee may have more opportunity for "managed" development through the Talent Steering Committee or other Human Resources initiative, they should not just rest on that assumption and wait for training or development opportunities to be offered to them. In some cases, the opportunities offered are not of interest to the individual (i.e., rotational assignments). Since the high performing employee list changes often, the individual may or may not know that they have been removed from the list for one reason or another. Either way, utilizing self-development as part of your ongoing personal initiatives is important whether or not you are identified as a high potential employee. Only you know what your end goal is and only you can create that plan to make it happen.

CHAPTER 13

Best Practices

I n this chapter, I plan to take specific areas of best practices and list out what I have seen that has worked well throughout my career. This is by no means an exhaustive listing, but should serve as a reminder of where all Project Managers and leaders need to pay close attention to the details.

Training:

- Onboarding training is vital to new team members and providing the roadmap of where organizational information is located and how to access it is critical to the success of the new hire and/or the newly transferred employee.
- Aligning training by job level or job description helps ensure that your team member is receiving the right training for their specific role. This should be an annual exercise for the manager to review their employees' training records and confirm that not only are the right training programs in place, but that all the training is being taken by that employee as expected.
- Training materials should be up to date and accurate, plus a centralized repository should be available for team members to access the training materials they need.
- If the company is open to it, request that Core Team Training be made available, or better yet, mandatory, for all new hires,

regardless of function, if they will be expected to be on a Core Team for a New Product Development project. This will guarantee that the new team members understand any existing Product Development Process, guidance and governance expectations along with a solid outline of how the Core Teams are expected to function.

Communications:

- You really cannot overcommunicate, and easily 80% of the Project Manager role is communications to begin with, so be sure to take time at the end of each day to review what you did and remind yourself who else needs to know that information so that you can get the information out to those who need it.
- Know your audience, and use the right medium to put the information out to them. Not everyone is interested in the same detail level of information. Know who is receiving the information and what level of detail is needed. At the higher levels of management, too much detail or too wordy of an email will quickly get deleted.
- Review each email before you send it out, not just for spelling and grammar, but for content. When you review for Who, What, Where, When and Why in your email, reading it as the receiver would, then you can be certain you have included all the correct content. How many times have you received an email telling you about an upcoming activity or request and it never listed the date when the activity or request was due? Or how many times did you receive (or send) an email that referenced an attachment that wasn't attached?
- Make "follow-up" a priority for yourself. Your overall reputation is mainly based on perception. Most people will interact with you only a few times, and if there is something they are expecting from you such as information, a return email, an individual's information, etc., they will absolutely remember how quickly you got that information to them and that you made them feel like a priority

too. This should not be limited to someone's "level" – treat every request the same and follow through on your commitments regardless of who is receiving the information.

- Have the project team speak with One Voice. Having the entire team on the same page regarding what information is released helps everyone to know the exact status and the needs of the project. When individual team members go to their cross functional leaders with sidebar stories and complaints, this can completely disrupt the progress of the Core Team. Gaining agreement up front from the Core Team members regarding what information is released, will benefit the project and the team members in the end.
- Provide an escalation path for the project issues and make sure everyone knows what that escalation path is and how to access it. Similar to the One Voice concept above, having the project team as a group agree to any necessary escalation will show that the team is aligned and united in their request for support either from their functional leaders or from the project governance team.

Governance and Prioritization:

- Governance and prioritization of projects is not just an annual event. Introduce the governance and prioritization team to the concept of an "evergreen model". Simply put, evergreen in this context means always reviewed and always up to date. Governance should be scheduled on a regular basis for the projects to inform on their Project Contract status and any escalation needs. Prioritization is just as critical due to rapidly changing technologies and/or simply roadblocks that can happen suddenly with the projects. This constant (evergreen) oversight will allow the governance team to make quick decisions and not throw money and resources to the wind working on a project that is no longer viable. This is a quick win for everyone, since you will surely be able to point out a project that went on far beyond its expiration point and analyze and report on the amount of money and resource hours that could have been saved or redirected to another project.

- Since the Governance team usually consists of the highest-level Vice Presidents and Division Presidents in the company, don't automatically assume that they have a good understanding of the existing Product Development Process and know what to look for with projects entering or exiting phases. It's helpful to create cheat sheets, explaining the key expectations and/or what to look for with a project entering or exiting a specific phase. Phase entry or phase exit questions are always a great idea, and having these laminated and available to the governance team members is usually very well received.

- Expect and be prepared for resistance with introducing project prioritization. The perception is correct that introducing prioritization and governance to projects and the overall portfolio will remove the existing control that a few individuals may have today over these projects. Once the project information is openly available, there may be some anger that information was hidden or that personal agendas may have been involved in keeping a specific project alive. Be objective and stay focused on the needs of the company. The work you are doing is only being done to benefit the consumer (or patient depending on the industry you work in) and the company's financial bottom line. As long as you remain objective about the data, then there can be no accusation that you are introducing this new prioritization process for any reason other than the stated company goals.

For Your Team:

- Create and adhere to operating mechanisms within your group or team. The larger the team is, the more important this becomes. When individuals know what your expectations are as a leader or as a Project Manager, then they will know how to meet those expectations. Operating Mechanisms can include staff meetings, status update templates or meetings, deep dives, town hall meetings, one on one meetings and skip level meetings. There should be no surprises to anyone who supports you as to what you need from them, when you will meet with them, and what information they need to provide to you on a regular basis.

- Make every effort to provide the necessary tools that your team members need. Whether this is software, training or general information, taking the time to know what support is necessary, and then helping to make that happen, is what every employee wants from their manager and what every team wants from their Project Manager.

- Learn how to listen. Don't zone out, stay focused on the conversations that you have with your team members. Not everyone wants you to do something about their complaints – sometimes they just want to vent and want you to listen – to be aware of a situation that is occurring. I've always had difficulty deciphering whether or not an individual wanted me to fix a problem or just hear them out. In those cases, I simply ask them, "do you need me to work on this or do you just want me to be aware"? I've often been surprised at the answer.

For you:

- Save yourself a tremendous amount of work at the end of the year doing your performance review by scheduling one hour during the last week of each month just for you to notate the items you worked on during that month. Make this a recurring appointment for yourself that you do not reschedule. During this hour, go back over your calendar and your inbox and just quickly type into a Word document all the items you worked on this past month. At the end of the year, this becomes your performance review roadmap and you can cull through the document to pick out only those items you wish to include as part of your performance appraisal input. Time saving isn't the only benefit to this trick – there are many things that you don't think twice about that had a major impact on your team or on a cross-functional team that you may have worked on. Taking this time for yourself each month ensures that you capture all of your hard work and efforts. Encourage your staff to do the same!

- Finding work life balance is one of the more difficult things for many leaders to manage. I've always found that this ebbs and flows depending on what is going on at a given time, but it's way too easy to get caught up in the day to day work and work too many hours and miss out on too many family events because of it. It took me awhile to figure it out, but I learned that taking an hour on a Sunday night (after everyone was asleep), to look at my work week in advance and plan for the week was extremely helpful. Additionally, during the week, if I did have an opportunity or need to put in an extra hour or two in the evening, I would usually schedule the emails I composed to be sent the following morning. This way I did not interrupt any of my team members personal time or make anyone feel like they had to respond to me outside of normal business hours. If that need were to ever arise, and it did, there would be a phone call instead.

- Be fair with everyone, and be your authentic self – individuals see through a phony manager very quickly.

- Put the same expectations on yourself that you do on your staff.

- Keep your stakeholders informed and maintain alignment through frequent and informative meetings. They often have great ideas and when you have the opportunity to implement one of their ideas, giving them full credit, you will have a solid partner.

- Demonstrating your anger gets you nothing but a bad reputation as a difficult person to deal with. I prefer to keep people guessing and to keep myself in complete control. I will admit to getting angry at work when I was younger, and had a great boss that sat in the office next to me and overheard one of my private tirades after I hung up from a rather unpleasant call. I remember hearing him say "Hey Marks", and I replied with an exasperated "What"? He asked if I got paid this week? I said "Yes". And then he said, "So shut the hell up then"! In the middle of my anger I was pretty stunned at what he said, and then I started to laugh. It was his way of reminding me that ultimately, I got a paycheck for the work I did and to take it easy on others and myself. The same goes for stress, we all have it at some level or another, but asking yourself if what you are doing right now will affect anyone or be known 100 years from now – is a sure-fire way to take a breath and wonder what you are getting so upset about.

- Finally, take responsibility and be accountable for your actions and decisions. We all make mistakes – learn from them. Apologize and move on, but don't try to blame someone else for your decision or your action. It was your call, own it. People will respect you for having the guts to admit when you're wrong.

CHAPTER 14

LEADERSHIP & POLITICS

There are so many books available on Leadership, that my going into depth here wouldn't make a dent in your philosophy or beliefs about what is the right Leadership style. There is no right style, it can be situational or it can be spontaneous. Is it nature versus nurture? Is the leader born a leader or bred into a leader with training? I believe it is a combination of both but for the purposes of this book the bottom line is what is your style, and how do you find out what it is? How do you use your leadership style to your benefit? Just as critical – what is the leadership style best supported by the culture of the company that you are working for?

It's important to become aware of and understand your leadership style, and your challenges, as early as possible in your career. You want to be able to correct, or at least modify your approach to certain situations (or people) quickly, and you can only do that when you know your own strengths and weaknesses. A Project Manager absolutely has to know their style, and how to modify it if necessary, to work with and lead teams. A PMO Leader needs an even better view of their style since they need to be flexible enough to lead both people and teams while interacting heavily with senior leadership.

By now you've likely worked for multiple managers, perhaps have even had a mentor or two along the way. Regardless, you've already seen what a good manager can do by way of leadership, motivation and cultivating talent. You've likely also seen how devastating a poor manager can be and the effects of a subpar leader on a team or on you personally.

I remember a course I had in college in Human Resources, and the text book indicating that 90% of the time employees leave managers, not the company. I found that statement very hard to believe, but in the years that have passed, I've seen it play out more times than I can count. Most employees won't say it at the time they are leaving, either because they don't want to burn the bridge or just out of personal integrity, but the truth is that more often than not, it is completely true. I have certainly left companies because of a bad manager in the past.

One of my recurring statements to my mentees is that you learn as much from a poor manager as you do from a good one. I stand by that, having had multiple poor (and I'm being exceptionally kind using the term poor) managers over the course of my career. Every time I worked for someone who was a terrible manager, I knew what I didn't want to be, I knew what I could never do in a leadership capacity, and most importantly, I knew that I never wanted an employee to feel about me the way I felt about that manager.

As noted earlier, you want to understand your leadership style early in your career. Why is that? Because once your leadership style is identified, it is unlikely to change at its core. What you can change is how people perceive your style, how they react to it and how you change your reactions to have a more acceptable style. But at your core, your beliefs, your values, your first instincts – they don't change, and when you know that, it's so much easier to be comfortable in learning how to work with and control your reactions.

Let's take the Myers-Briggs personality type survey, which I have taken about 6 times in my career as it falls in and out of favor at companies over the years. Each and every time my results were the same – this over a 30-year period of time. If you are familiar with Myers-Briggs, you answer the many questions and get a 4-letter indicator as a result. I was consistently ENTJ –pegged to the far end of the spectrum every time, always the same. While it was interesting to learn what each of the letters meant, it later became more fascinating to learn what my results meant when interacting with any of the other possible 16 Myers-Briggs outcomes and how they perceived my ENTJ persona. As a side note, I once had a manager who assigned projects based on her team members individual Myers-Briggs results.

At the time I thought it very odd, but once she understood what the project needed, she knew exactly who to assign to it, and who would succeed with that project based on their personality type. She was never wrong, but in time it became redundant being assigned to the same type of projects all the time. Essentially, she hurt her Project Managers by not letting them grow and try other types of projects. However, from a corporate perspective, she was deemed quite successful since all the projects assigned to her group were ultimately very successful.

An ENTJ Myers-Briggs outcome stands for:

E = Extrovert
N = Intuitive
T = Thinking
J = Judging

The one that surprised me most was the Extrovert. I am by nature clearly not an extrovert and do not enjoy being the center of attention. I will take center stage if I have to, and will lead and manage meetings and do speaking engagements and no one will ever recognize that I'm not comfortable with it nor does this come naturally to me. But when it was explained to me that the Extrovert means that I get my motivating externally, from others, then it all made absolute sense. Yes, I am motivated by others and am not motivated internally by my own needs. I will truly push myself to the limit to meet other's expectations but would happily sit all day and read a good book if left to my own internal desires.

The next indicator was Intuitive, which I agree with, and that comes with experience. But I always recommend that you trust your gut instincts within limits. While I've surely been burned by my instincts in the past, especially interviewing candidates for roles in my organization, I have by far, at least 10 times over, been more successful in trusting my own instincts when it came to serious decisions. The opposing term is S for Sensing on this personality trait.

The Thinking trait is more my style versus the opposite trait which is defined with an F for Feeling. And the Judging trait? No doubt about it! I am judgmental to a fault which I recognize and work hard to move to the opposing P indicator, which is Perceiving.

If you have not done the Myers-Briggs on yourself, I do recommend that you take the test and read about your specific outcome. Additionally, you want to know how you relate to and are perceived by others, and there are many resources available online and in books that will help you to learn how others perceive you once you know your personal style.

From my outcome, I know I can be perceived as demanding, overwhelming and certainly seen as "in charge". I do not disagree with any of those terms, but being defined by those terms is not what a genuine leader wants. The ideal outcome is to know these traits exist, know how individuals can perceive you, and learn how to flex your style to meet the needs of the situation.

Among other personality and leadership style tests I've found helpful and interesting, is the Keirsey Temperament Scanner. This was a fun and helpful exercise that was done across a large group of Project Managers as a team building exercise. Which, following the discussion of the outcomes, broke everyone up into their preferred style groups for some enlightening and enjoyable comparisons.

While there is a myriad of different types of tests, including 360 degree feedback tests given to co-workers or stakeholders and other in-depth personality self-administered tests often provided by Search Firms or Executive Recruiters, my point is that you should take the time to look inward, to understand your preferences, reactions and overall style. Each of these tools have many websites and books associated with them to give you all the details, and you need to find what's best for you and research it. Ultimately, people perceive you in a certain way, and that perception is their reality. Whether others perceptions of you are accurate or not, it is what you are up against – and the more you understand yourself and your style, the easier it will be to work with others and to flex your style to get what you need from all of your interactions.

Understanding your style will also help you to navigate through the politics that exist in your work environment. And every company has them. Politics are about power, who has it and who doesn't. The higher you go in the organization, the less you can avoid playing the game. And a game it is – someone once told me that "at the end of the day, when you walk out of this building, your level doesn't matter, we are all the same – we all put our pants on one leg at a time". They had it right – and when you learn to play the game, which includes understanding your role in it, then you get the opportunity to move up and win.

I truly believe your leadership style needs to be aligned to the culture of the company that you work for. By this I mean that an aggressive leadership style may work very well in one company, but you would not be successful in the kinder or gentler company environments! This was a hard-learned lesson for me previously, as I had come from a very aggressive company culture and moved into a company with a very kind and considerate culture. I came on too strong, and with the assistance of a very astute HR partner, was told to tone it back 100% or I wouldn't last three months in this new role. She was right, and it was very hard for me to take the time that was needed to go and build relationships with each stakeholder and get buy-in on each and every item I wanted to implement. Yet in that specific company culture, it was the only way it would work.

So ultimately it becomes a balancing act of knowing your personal leadership style and your company's culture. A good Project Manager is a chameleon, knowing how to flex their style to work well with their team. A great leader is also a chameleon, the difference being that the successful leader <u>has to</u> understand and flex their style with the politics involved at their level along with managing their leadership style with their employees.

CLOSING

E arly on in this book I indicated, and want to reiterate, that a PMO is a cyclical organization. On a 3 to 5-year cycle, a PMO can go from a centralized to a decentralized organization and then back to centralized again in another 3-5 years. There is very little you can do about it, because it depends on the corporate leadership at the time and the overall perceived value of, and the need for, the PMO. Tools and processes may change, but the need for a solid Project Manager to bring a project in on time and in scope and budget, never changes. A passionate and skilled Project Manager is worth their weight in gold to a company. The real question is whether or not the company sees and appreciates that skill set!

In hindsight, I look at my career as a series of choices I made and chances that I took along the way. A few were mistakes, I easily acknowledge that – but I learned from them. I learned that Marketing was not my thing and that I couldn't sell anything if I tried. I found out that I could push myself to learn new technologies and systems that no one thought I could master, and that I was motivated by the fact that people thought I couldn't do it, which made me try even harder to prove them wrong. I've learned that people can be very kind and people can be very cruel, to keep my personal life to myself at work and hold my family and friends close at home. Above all, the words my mother told me from a young age turned out to be the best leadership advice I've ever received; Treat others as you wish to be treated – and be fair about it. I would not do for one person what I would not do for every member of my team, and my team always knew that was the case. I didn't play favorites, I gave credit where credit was due and I always had my team members' backs. The regrets I had are long forgotten, since I can't change those situations anyway and they are well in the past now. We all move on and shouldn't look back with regret or sadness, only forward with anticipation.

As I now move out of the full time corporate world and into Consulting and Speaking engagements, I am excited to assist those Project Managers and forward-thinking companies who value the Project Management principles and processes and want to reap the benefits of a strong PMO with aligned Portfolio Management. Following 35 years in the corporate world, from minor Medical Device companies to large pharmaceutical and major telecommunications giants, I am still surprised at how many of the common tenets of good Project Management exist across all these companies and industries, and I doubt that is going to change anytime soon.

My sincere thanks to you for taking the time to read this book and to consider the ideas and methodologies included within. My Consulting company is Peak Method Consulting, and the website is https://pmo. method.cloud. Your questions and comments are welcome, and you can reach me at my email karen@pmo.method.cloud. I would love to hear your feedback on the book!

Best of Luck!

Coming in 2018! My Next Book - "Let's Fix This Project!"

I'm happy to announce that I have already begun work on my next book, entitled "Let's Fix this Project!"; Tactics and Techniques to Restore Project Health. This book will go into deep detail on the many reasons why projects fail and how to correct these issues early. I'm hopeful that this new book will be available by mid-2018. Following is the Preface to the new book:

All Project Managers know that no two projects are created equal. Projects inherently have varying needs depending on the make-up of the project deliverables and the skills of the individual project team members. Every project faces challenges, however, some may seem to be insurmountable and can put the project so far behind schedule that it takes a herculean effort to put the project back on track.

This book will address the multiple ways to bring a project back into alignment. If senior leadership has lost confidence in the team or if the team has lost confidence in the project, there are many ways to reassess and realign the project efforts and bring the project back under control.

I write from the perspective of both a Project Manager and as a Senior Leader, having had unique experiences in both roles and with more than a few failed projects under my belt as well as many successful high value projects. The methods I detail in the book are more than just theory, these are actual tried and tested techniques which I have personally utilized.

While no one can guarantee any project will be successful, there is a level of commitment that is expected from the team at the inception of the project that calls for every avenue to be explored to find a solution to the project issues before it is too late. In most cases, a significant amount of resources, both financial and people, has already been invested in the project and in the case of public companies, preliminary information may have already been provided to investors to get them excited about upcoming products. We owe it to the team, to our stakeholders and our investors, to take every opportunity to get to a successful project outcome.

CPSIA information can be obtained
at www.ICGtesting.com
Printed in the USA
BVHW04s0816230318
511396BV00014B/230/P

9 780692 939079